[signature]

A Place Called Home
Moments from an ordinary life

by

Craig Nagel

authorHOUSE®

AuthorHouse™
1663 Liberty Drive, Suite 200
Bloomington, IN 47403
www.authorhouse.com
Phone: 1-800-839-8640

First published by AuthorHouse 8/28/2007

ISBN: 978-1-4343-2285-2 (e)
ISBN: 978-1-4343-2286-9 (sc)

Library of Congress Control Number: 2007904657

Printed in the United States of America
Bloomington, Indiana

This book is printed on acid-free paper.

The cover of this book is a watercolor titled "Northern Lights II" by Stephanie Mirocha, Aitkin, MN, and is used with permission of the artist.

Dedication

This book is for my mother, Marie Carol Nagel, and in memory of my father, Wilbur "Spike" Nagel, who together taught me the bewitching art of reading and encouraged me to approach the world with a sense of joy and curiosity. Thank you from the core of who I am.

Contents

Preface

In 1972 I was hired to start a weekly newspaper. The owners named it *The Country Echo*. Shortly after getting the paper underway, I bought controlling interest and ran it for the next several years. Later I sold it and turned my hand to other endeavors.

In 1981 the new owners invited me to start writing a biweekly column for the paper, which I've been doing ever since. I titled it "The Cracker Barrel," after the barrel in which crackers were kept in country stores and around which customers lounged for informal conversation. I wanted it to be suggestive of the friendly homespun character of an old-fashioned general store, with nothing too shrill or subversive.

All of the essays in this book were originally written for "The Cracker Barrel." To put them in some sort of perspective, I've interspersed them along with a brief narrative of my life.

As lives go, mine has been rather ordinary. I've neither scaled the pinnacle of great accomplishment nor, with one exception, stumbled through the valley of unbearable heartache. Instead I've had the good fortune to live, in the main, a life of quiet joy, accompanied most of the way by a loving family and a wide variety of interesting friends.

One of my greatest satisfactions has come from sharing stories and ideas with readers like you. I hope you'll find what follows worthy of your consideration.

Craig Nagel

Pequot Lakes, Minnesota

Spring 2007

Narrative

I was born in Chicago, Illinois, and my earliest memories of the city are uniformly pleasant, except for the fact that my father had to go away to WWII just about the time I was starting to talk. When he came back on furlough, I recall being upset by the strange man in our house. But he pulled a red toy car from his duffle bag and gave it to me, and after that we got along fine.

During those tumultuous war years, life as I remember it was pretty laid back. A popcorn vendor pushed his cart up the street once a week and we kids would run to the curb, a nickel clutched in our sweaty palms, to transact our business. Back then a nickel bag meant popcorn, not dope. Other weekly highlights included listening to Fibber McGee on the radio, going to the fire station down the block (where the firemen would take you upstairs and give you a ride down the brass sliding pole and let you sit in the cab of the hook-and-ladder truck), and going to church and lighting candles to bring Dad and all the others safely back from the war.

Every so often we'd load up the car and drive out to Grandpa's cottage in the little town of Long Lake, 50 miles north of the city. Those weekends remain, in memory, occasions of singular pleasure. After the war my parents bought the cottage from Grandpa and remodeled it into a permanent home, and when I was midway through the first grade we moved out of the city into the country.

Weekend Magic

When I was very young, weekends were a time of magic. World War II was being fought and all the talk was about death and the fear that someone wouldn't return and how hard it was to get meat and coffee and sugar. Being a child, I didn't pay much attention to the specifics of adult concerns—but I vividly remember the feel of things, and how every so often someone would just start crying, bam!, right out of the blue.

But weekends were different.

On weekends, when finances and weather permitted, we would pile in the car and drive north from Chicago to Grandpa's summer place at Long Lake.

A few miles before we got there we would stop at a diner and pick up a cardboard carton of hot breaded shrimp. The aroma would make you whimper with anticipation.

At the cabin, the old pot-bellied stove with the isinglass windows would soon start driving the chill out of the place, and as the warmth spread we would settle in around the stove and commence our assault on the shrimp. Grandpa would uncap a couple of quart bottles of Blatz beer and a motley assortment of glasses would blossom with foam, and a feeling of safekeeping and joy would fill the little house.

Later the games would begin. Poker, for sure, and pinochle. There may have been others, but I remember those two most clearly. The poker chips fascinated me, and I recall being spanked and sent prematurely to bed for slipping chips to someone under the table.

The table was covered with oilcloth and over it hung a big stained-glass lamp. For hours the slap of cards and the clatter of chips would mix with the laughter; belly-deep man-laughter and higher, trilling woman-laughter; laughter that contrasted magically from the hushed worry of the weekdays.

Once in a while there'd be an argument, usually between my two grandmothers, generally over a pinochle score. But the disagreements were short-lived and always followed by more laughter.

On Saturday nights the routine varied slightly. Instead of shrimp there would be sandwiches, thick concoctions made of German rye bread piled with ham and cheese and mustard, accompanied by a jar of big dill pickles. And always there was laughter, jokes and smiles and laughter, and it made such an impression on me that I came to think of it as magic.

Then a global war was raging and matters were literally of life and death. Now the war is limited but there are still worries, all sorts of worries, because life is always well stocked with worries, even in the best of times.

But the magic is still accessible.

All it takes is time and the willingness to come together to have fun.

Grandpa's House

As a small child I spent a lot of time with my grandparents. Dad was in Germany fighting Hitler's forces on the Western Front, and Mom, of necessity, had to work.

My maternal grandparents lived on the north side of Chicago in a one-story house with a side porch and a modest fenced yard, at the back of which sat a garage that gave onto an alley.

To a passerby, Grandpa's place was probably unremarkable. The house was covered with asphalt siding formed to look like bricks. I remember the trim was nicely painted and the yard was kept mowed and the garden weeded; otherwise there wasn't much to reach out and grab your attention. But to a small boy's imagination, the place was like a fairy-tale palace.

For starters, there was the stained-glass window set into the sidewall of the living room, above and to the left of the never-used gas fireplace. If you waited until the sun hit it just right, the window sent beams of magical light down onto the carpet; blues and reds and yellows that turned the skin on the back of your hand into something a Martian would envy and transformed a blank piece of paper into a rainbow.

Once the sun had shifted and the magic light was gone, you could spend some time studying Grandma's parakeet, a gorgeous green creature with a yellow head named Skippy, who whiled away the hours swinging on a little bar in his cage and kept to himself unless you tried to feed him a seed, whereupon he would peck at your fingers. As I recall, his vocabulary was rather limited, consisting mainly of squawks and whistles and the words "pretty boy," which he repeated several hundred times a day and which, I presume, expressed his own rather immodest opinion of himself.

If Grandma was baking bread, you could join her in the kitchen and help punch down the dough, or scoop some flour in your bare hands from the tilt-out bin in the cupboard and sprinkle it over the counter when she was ready to flatten stuff out with the rolling pin. Fifty years later I still see her with floured arms, a white smudge on her forehead from pushing an errant hair back into place; a wonderfully warm person with laughing brown eyes wearing a checkered apron and a ready smile. On the rare occasion when something upset her, she would shake her head and mutter, "Aw, pshaw." I remember that because I practiced saying it, thinking it was a swear word.

Once in a while she would send me to fetch something from the attic, which was roughly the equivalent of going to the moon. The stairway was piled on both sides with seasonal things like galoshes and Christmas ornaments and hatboxes, and presented a challenge to young legs. But the effort of clambering up those steep stairs was nothing compared to the terrors of the attic itself. In the dim light you encountered dust-laden trunks big enough to hide a corpse, boxes of all sizes containing who knows what, the roughly-laid brick chimney that rose through the forest of rafters and rasped your skin if you brushed against it, and, horror of horrors, the curtain stretchers.

Children of today are spared the sight of curtain stretchers, and consequently have no genuine sense of fear. But to the young of yesteryear, the shadowy framework glinting with the needle sharp points of a thousand nails was enough to cause permanent mental trauma. You imagined yourself impaled on those piranha teeth and stretched to paper thinness while some twisted monster fashioned you into a lampshade. It was enough to make a boisterous boy whimper, and no lectures about "behaving" were necessary once your eyes had glimpsed those evil rows of nails.

The terrors of the attic, however, were more than offset by the marvels in the basement. It was here, safe in the lap of mother earth, that a child's fancy could grow serious roots.

The basement was divided in half, one part devoted to laundry, the other to heat (or, on a more ancient and poetic level, water and fire). The laundry room had a double sink big enough to drown in, a wringer washing machine with rollers that, I was warned, could double the size of your hand while reducing its thickness in half, and overhead drying lines festooned with dozens of clothespins. The room smelled of damp clay and chlorine bleach (which I took for the tang of saltwater) and conjured up fantasies of naval adventures, the clotheslines serving as the rigging of a ship and the thick wooden posts supporting the floor above as masts.

When you tired of playing pirate you could step through the opening to the back part of the basement, in the center of which sat a squat round furnace with a hungry mouth and tendrils of ductwork that snaked around the ceiling like the arms of a giant octopus. The furnace ate coal by the shovelful and, with its front door open, coughed out blasts of heat like a fire-breathing dragon. If you turned off the overhead lights and squinted, you could imagine something alive; a monster with glowing orange eyes and a row of red teeth. It gave off a peculiar dusty smell of vaporized coal and refried sheet metal. You didn't dare get too close to the thing for fear of melting, but you knew it kept everything warm. A monster, maybe, but a friendly one.

Grandpa's basement held other excitements, like the mountain of glittering black nuggets in the coal bin and the partitioned-off room that held an old desk and had once been used as some sort of office. The big workbench next to that boasted a huge green vise and tin cans of nails and, above it, a row of tools, each hanging in its designated spot. In the shadows cast by the bare light bulbs, all things were magical and full of shape-shifting possibilities. I never tired of going to Grandpa's house and can recall no moments of boredom there.

When Grandma died, Grandpa decided to sell the place and follow his son and daughters out of the city. The property was bought by a neighborhood business. The house was torn down, the basement filled in, and the earth sealed over with blacktop to make a parking lot.

Since then several decades have ticked away, and I still can't get my mind to accept that the magical house is gone.

But, in one way at least, it isn't.

I discovered long ago that I can go back there whenever I want, to gaze in terror at the curtain stretchers or happily storm the seas in my basement pirate ship.

All I have to do is close my eyes and remember.

Narrative

For a boy who grew to love swimming and fishing and camping and playing baseball, life in a small town in the '50s was close to perfect. Being near Chicago added an extra layer of adventure. Seventy cents would get you a ride on the commuter train all the way in to Union Station. For twenty cents more you could get on a city bus and go to Wrigley Field to watch the Cubs, visit the zoo at Lincoln Park, enjoy thrills and chills at Riverview Amusement Park, view Egyptian mummies at the Field Museum of Natural History, or walk through a captured German submarine at the Science Museum nearby. Looking back, I'd say we had the best of both worlds.

Freak Shows

One of the most powerful and unpleasant memories I tote around from childhood dates back to the mid-fifties and involves a young man known as the Seal Boy.

I was 11 or 12, and had taken the commuter train into Chicago from our little hometown of Long Lake, some 50 miles north of the city. There were four or five of us, all guys my age, and we were in very high spirits. It was summertime, school was a distant memory, and we were finally going to Riverview Park, a big amusement complex on the north side of town.

As I recall, we all had a wonderful time for the first several hours. We went on the roller coaster and the tilt-a-whirl and rode the boat down the shoot-the-chute. We gorged ourselves on hot dogs and pop and cotton candy and won a few prizes knocking things over with baseballs. We groped our way through the pitch-blackness of the Fun House and nearly died of laughter watching ourselves in the distorting mirrors.

Then we went into the Freak Show.

Such shows were common years back, and nobody seemed to think it wrong to put people with hideous physical deformities on public display. We paid our 25-cent admission and stepped inside to see the Fat Lady (who was said to weigh well over 600 pounds) and the Siamese Twins (two girls whose bodies were joined together from hip to shoulder) and The Dwarf (a grown man less than four feet tall). Being the sensitive and caring souls we were, we hooted and hollered with great glee.

But the hilarity stopped when we saw the Seal Boy.

The Seal Boy looked to be the same age we were. He wore a crew cut and jeans with the cuffs rolled up, just like we did. He was of average height with dark brown eyes. He stood on display in his little booth, bare-chested, so everyone could see that his hands grew directly out of his shoulders, like the flippers of a seal.

Our eyes caught, and for one indelible instant I could see the longing and the sadness as he stared out at someone his own age who could play catch and swing a bat and shoot marbles and pet a dog. Then I dropped my gaze, turned, and walked away, my own eyes filled with tears.

Nowadays, of course, the notion of displaying deformities is out of favor, and the idea of a freak show strikes us as repulsive.

Or does it?

I am no watcher of TV talk shows, but from what I gather they're steadily booked with freaks of the mental and emotional sort. And millions of Americans spend parts of each day taking a perverse sort of pleasure watching them. The more outrageous the behavior, the better. The greater the deformities, the higher the entertainment value.

Have we no shame?

Looking Back

One of the givens of life is that the older you get, the harder your childhood becomes.

Not too many years ago I was rolling my eyes and thinking skeptical thoughts as my father reminisced about the length and severity of his grammar-school-era paper route, and how he had to rise at five in the morning in order to finish the route before attending class.

Now, a few decades later, his claims no longer seem exaggerated; not when you compare them with life as it was lived when we were kids. For those of us who grew up in the '40s, '50s, '60s and '70s, the world bristled with sharp edges and offered little in the way of padding.

For starters, our baby cribs were covered with bright-colored lead-based paint. We didn't have childproof lids on medicine bottles. If a thermometer broke, we got to play with the mercury, rolling the little ball of quicksilver around the floor or using it to restore tarnished pennies and dimes to a gleaming shine.

We rode in cars with no airbags and often no seatbelts. A lot of times we rode standing up in the front seat, relying on the driver to shoot out a restraining arm to keep us from crashing into the dashboard during a sudden stop. If we were rural and lucky, we got to ride in the back of the pickup truck along with the family dog.

Later we rode our bikes without wearing helmets, drank water from a garden hose instead of a store-bought bottle, made go-carts out of scraps and raced them downhill without benefit of brakes, turned green from smoking corn silk cigarettes or eating a worm on a bet, and weren't above stealing a tomato or melon from whomever's garden was ripest.

We would leave home in the morning as soon as chores were done and play all day, as long as we were back when supper was ready. In the absence of cell phones, we were unreachable for hours at a time. If someone needed us, they'd have to come looking.

We played dodge ball and sometimes the ball hurt like hell. We played scratch football and hockey without protective equipment and got cuts and broken bones and chipped teeth and there were no lawsuits from these accidents. They were just accidents, with no one to blame but ourselves. We had fights and punched each other and got black and blue and learned to get over it.

We ate cupcakes and Twinkies and spoonfuls of peanut butter and drank Kool-Aid loaded with sugar, but nobody was badly overweight because we were constantly playing outside, running and hiking and swimming and biking and sledding, and nothing was motorized. We shared a soda pop with friends, everybody drinking from the same bottle, and nobody died.

We didn't have PlayStation, Nintendo 64, X-box, 99 channels of TV, videotape movies, surround sound, personal phones, computers, or Internet chat rooms. Instead we had friends. When we wanted to be with them we stood outside their house and yelled for them or knocked on the door or rang the bell or sometimes just walked inside. If they still had chores to do we helped them, knowing the sooner they were finished, the sooner we'd both be free to play. If we happened to be at a friend's house at lunchtime, chances are we ate there, helping ourselves to the food as if we were part of the family.

We made up games with sticks and tennis balls and fashioned scrap-wood swords and shot at each other with BB guns and although we were warned it could happen, we never put out an eye. Little League had tryouts and not everybody made the team. Those who didn't had to learn to deal with it. Some students weren't as smart as others so they failed a grade and were held back. Tests weren't adjusted for any reason, and if you got in trouble at school, your parents sided with the teacher.

Was the world back then a better place? Not necessarily. For most of those decades Americans were spooked about Commies. Racism was rampant. Women's rights were limited. Kids grew up scared of getting polio. And over it all hung the threat of nuclear war.

But on the personal front we did enjoy the benefits of common sense. Our actions were our own. Consequences were expected. You grew up knowing there was no one to hide behind and that, for better or worse, you were responsible for what you did. With few exceptions, right was right and wrong was wrong, and most everybody in the community agreed upon which was which. You got yelled at by whatever adult happened to see you doing something wrong, and encouraged by whomever saw you doing right.

Looking back, I'd say it was a pretty good time to be a kid, and I hope that someday soon we'll shake off the nonsense of coddling and scheduling and running interference for our young. Let them get on with the task of building their own lives, so that when they're older they, too, can brag about how tough it was to be a child.

Gettin' on Down

I was walking toward the dumpster at the job site, carrying a bucket of debris, when out of the corner of my eye I saw something green and shiny on the ground. I reached down and came up holding a marble, a perfect little ball of glass the color of lime Jell-O. When I held it toward the sun, I saw it was what in childhood we called a "purey," pure green throughout, as opposed to rainbows or cat's eyes or peppermint stripes.

Later that day I found myself smoothing off a little patch of ground, kneeling on one knee, and trying a few shots. To my surprise, the feel of the cool spring dirt under my knuckles brought back a wave of memories unvisited for the better part of forty years.

Suddenly I was back at the railroad station in Long Lake, Illinois, waiting with a couple dozen other kids for the school bus to come. It was a bright spring morning, the air was full of bird song, and a bunch of us were grouped around the hard-packed dirt between the station and the railroad track, getting ready to play marbles.

The way we played was not, I know now, quite up to official snuff. According to my trusty *World Book* encyclopedia, most kids play a game called ringer, in which a ten-foot diameter circle is scratched in the dirt, and 13 marbles are placed in a cross at the center of the circle. Each player then uses a larger marble (called the shooter) to knock or "shoot" the smaller marbles out of the ring, with the winner being whoever shoots the most marbles out.

We, instead, made a little depression at the center of the circle, which we called the hole. The hole was a place of sanctuary, and the object was to get your marble there without getting it shot by somebody else. If you hit the hole on your first shot, you got an extra turn, which gave you the chance to shoot at someone else's marble not yet in the hole.

We also played a variant game called bomber, in which you tried to hit the marbles on the ground by dropping your shooter from the air. And unlike the game described in the encyclopedia, in which the players play "for fair," returning all marbles to their original owners at the end of the game, we played "for keeps." If somebody hit your marble, it was his.

One nice thing about playing marbles was the low cost of getting outfitted. Every kid I knew had at least a coffee can full of marbles, and for the life of me I can't remember anyone ever buying any. Somehow you just ended up having as many marbles as you needed, which may have been an early object lesson in the idea of divine providence. Unlike Nintendo, you didn't have to manipulate your parents in order to play. And you didn't have to plug anything in or ever worry about batteries.

Whether you played with steelies or moonstones or mibs, marbles taught one valuable lesson indeed: the value of knuckling down. That's right: your dictionary will verify the fact. Mine puts it this way: "knuckling down—1.to place the knuckles on the ground preparatory to shooting a marble; 2.to apply oneself with concentration: to apply oneself earnestly."

So there. Little did we suspect that this rolling rite of spring was actually a preparation for one's grown-up years. And little did we care. All we knew was that when spring came, and the earth was moist and of just the right consistency, you scrounged up some marbles and got on down.

Sole Brothers

While shopping for shoes the other day I happened into conversation with an older gentleman also looking for footwear.

Neither of us was very enthused about the choices on display. The few pairs that struck my fancy would have required a second mortgage, and the rest (which comprised the great majority) consisted mainly of tennis shoes.

Evidently the Onward Rush of Progress had left us both in its wake, and the best we could do was commiserate about the changing times and harken back to days gone by.

"In my day," said the gentleman, "canvas shoes were reserved for two occasions. One, you had to wear them in physical education class, and two, you got to wear them in the summertime, when school was out.

"The rest of the time you wore your leather shoes, and God help you if you got them scuffed. I remember getting a little gash in the toe of my shoe once, and the way my father carried on you'd have thought the world was ending.

"We got one pair of shoes for the whole year back then, and it was understood that having them was both a privilege and a serious responsibility. On Saturday nights my brother and I would go down in the basement and polish our shoes for church the next day, and believe you me we put some elbow grease into the effort. First we'd clean all the dirt out of the seams with an old toothbrush, and then we'd go at it with the polish. Three coats we used to give 'em, and each coat we'd brush off with the old brush, then the new brush, and then the buffing rag. We had a bit of a contest, you see, trying to outdo one another. But, boy, did those shoes shine!"

I murmured assent, remembering my own evenings in the basement. But I didn't mention that I usually gave mine only one coat.

"And I remember the way it felt when school let out for the summer, and we got to take off our leather shoes and put the canvas ones on. Lord Almighty, how light and powerful it made you feel! It seemed like you were made of rubber bands and cotton, the way you could run and jump and leap such distances. When those astronauts landed on the moon and started hoppin' and glidin' around and carrying on about the gravity bein' so reduced, I knew exactly how they felt. But nowadays the kids wear lightweight shoes year-round, and never get the chance to feel such pleasure."

I was about to point out that maybe today's kids have the pleasure all the time, but just then his wife came along and trundled him off to look at some pillowcases, and I waved goodbye and said it was nice talking.

Then I went back to where the old-style sneakers were standing and spent a fine few minutes hefting one in each hand and remembering how I, too, had thrilled to the annual summer treat of unexpected buoyancy. And, remembering, I admitted to myself that the old gentleman was right.

A pleasure's not a pleasure if you have it all the time.

Narrative

By the time I was in high school, things were changing. The lake in which we swam and fished was closed to both activities, victim of rapid population growth and the absence of effective sewage treatment. Roads were increasingly clogged with traffic. Our beloved "bluff," an empty meadow on the edge of town where we'd earlier built Indian-style huts and whiled away whole days dreaming boyhood dreams, was subdivided into housing lots. Well-meaning adults erected playground equipment in the outfield of the baseball park, wrecking centerfield and part of left. Our corner of the world had fallen prey to progress. Perhaps not coincidentally, a friend handed me a copy of Thoreau's Walden. "Read this," he said. "It's kind of interesting."

In 1959 I went off to St. Olaf College in Northfield, Minnesota, which in retrospect marked the end of my Illinois citizenship. I came back summers and worked construction to pay for the next year's tuition, but my heart had abandoned the Land of Lincoln in favor of the North Star State. In the winter of both my junior and senior years, I volunteered for work in the canoe country at the end of the Gunflint Trail north of Lake Superior, dismantling log cabins during the day and hunkering around the barrel stove at night, reading by the light of a kerosene lantern. Someone in the group had discovered the magic of Sigurd Olson's books, and we devoured them. Olson's descriptions of life in the wilderness struck us as infinitely more exciting than life in more settled places.

Living, however briefly, beyond the lifeline of civilization (no electricity, no gas, no telephone) brought me alive in ways I'd never experienced. Working all day in pine-scented air, hearing no machine sounds save for an occasional plane overhead, walking two miles down the frozen Saganaga River at night to take a sauna in -35 degree temperatures was itself exciting; rounding a curving rock cliff and looking up to see a timber wolf silhouetted against a full moon brought unspeakable joy. By the end of the second trip to the wilderness, I knew I wanted to move to the woods.

After graduation I spent the summer working in Montana, returning to Illinois in time to get a provisional teaching certificate and teach eighth grade at a country school. I loved my students and was tempted to stay for a second year, but the lure of the woods proved too strong. I decided to spend the summer working on a horse ranch in southern Wisconsin, helping build miles of wooden fencing. Come autumn I'd migrate north.

One afternoon in late June, work done and leather gloves already tossed in the car, I noticed a roll of new barbed wire someone had left lying in the grass. Barehanded, I gingerly picked it up, started toward the barn—and promptly tripped over a gopher mound. The wire sliced a deep gash in the base of my thumb. An hour later, emerging from the doctor's office with a dozen stitches in my hand, I knew I'd be unable to hold a hammer for at least a couple of weeks. The next day I picked up my check at the ranch, piled a few boxes of books, a hatchet, a frying pan, a coffee pot, and an old ukulele in my car, said goodbye to my family, and set out for Minnesota. The die was cast. I would find a place in the woods.

What I wanted was an inexpensive place to park my few belongings and get on with the task at hand, which was to write "The Great American Novel." Classmates from college might go to graduate school or hire on with promising corporations; I would become a self-taught writer like my hero, John Steinbeck. The key to everything was to keep life simple, a la Thoreau. The goal, as best I could voice it, was to live authentically, by which I suppose I meant as directly from the land as possible. I would raise my own food, build my own shelter, burn my own firewood to keep warm. The only question was where.

I started by renting an old log cabin on the shore of a small lake west of Bemidji. The cabin was built of huge white pine logs, four to each wall, and had originally served as the cook shack in a turn-of-the-century logging camp. I spent the days hiking through the woods and looking at parcels of land for sale, and scribbled away at my writing after dark. Summer gave way to fall and my heart soared at the beauty of the autumnal woods framed by ceramic blue skies. I began meeting people whose lives were very different from my own: trappers, loggers, fishing guides, subsistence farmers; known locally as "jack pine savages." On one memorable Greyhound trip down to Minneapolis, I was introduced to the mysteries of Ojibwe beadwork by an old furrow-faced man in the back of the bus whose gnarled brown fingers patiently traced the patterns of the beads as he explained their significance.

Gentle Reminders

It's been nearly forty years since I moved here to the woods, yet the details of those early days remain vital and vivid in my mind.

Accustomed to the blowtorch heat of Illinois, I found the days here most bearable and the evenings a delight. Weary of urban frenzy, I decided to regulate my life by inner, rather than outer, devices. I put away my clock and wristwatch and let my body decide when it wanted to eat, when it needed sleep, when it felt like lying in the sun instead of working.

At first it seemed I slept two-thirds of every day. But gradually the fatigue subsided and was replaced by a growing sense of wonder and intrigue. I roamed the woods for hours on end, enthralled by the smells and sights and sounds that impressed themselves upon me. I felt like a castaway exploring an uncharted island. Everything seemed freshly created, mysterious, pulsing with an inner power.

With the help of friends I learned to distinguish red pine from white, chickadee from nuthatch, northern from walleye. Little by little I made sense of strange phrases like "working out" (as in leaving the homestead in order to make money) and "going ricing," and came to understand that Sorels and choppers were articles of clothing.

As summer faded into fall, I felt an unprecedented excitement building in my brain. I had always loved fall; but here it promised to be extraordinary. With the cooling nights came the distant howl of coyotes and a sky shot through with stars. During the day, the sky seemed impossibly blue, as if the air itself had been dyed. Yellow leaves began floating down from the birches and popples around my cabin, rocking like miniature boats on the water at my beach, gentle reminders that life moves in sweeping circles, not in straight lines.

Labor Day weekend came and passed and the roads and lakes were suddenly unoccupied. I took to walking for entire days, meandering cross-country, discovering potholes, napping on hilltops, flushing grouse, watching awestruck the first time I saw a pileated woodpecker at work. In the cabin at night I would write the day's events into my journal, along with comments and questions and the ponderings natural to a young man unsure of his future.

Was it wise (I would write) to leave the familiar and come up here to the unknown? Was it sensible to turn away from the opportunities the city offered and come to a place where jobs were scarce and wages low? Did peace and beauty and purity of environment really matter more than career success?

The next day I would be reassured by those gentle messengers, the yellow leaves.

"Life is short," they seemed to whisper. "Life is to be smelled and stroked and sipped and savored. Life is best when it is simple and comes straight through your senses. Don't trade too much of your time for dollars. Money isn't life."

Once again I would find myself at peace.

The Humility Bead

For many of us, the quest for perfection began in the cradle. From infancy on, we were taught to believe that anything short of perfection somehow constitutes failure.

Examples of this sort of thing are everywhere; in the classroom, on the playing field, in the home, even in the church. Adults set up standards of expectation—and anything that departs from those standards means (to the child's mind) disgrace. A young boy goes out for Little League baseball, makes the starting team, and promptly drops the first ball hit to him. What does he hear? Groans, catcalls, insults—sometimes from his own father or mother.

Americans want to be first. We put a very high premium on winning. Sure, we talk about the importance of sportsmanship or playing by the rules or being nice. But when the chips are down most of us try mightily to insure that we come out on top.

Which, in one sense, is as it should be. Why shoot for second best? Why not go for the gold?

In a direct head-to-head competition, it makes sense to try to be first. The danger, however, is that we come to believe that all situations call for this sort of effort, when in fact they do not. Contemporary anthropologists have begun to reassess the notion that man is by nature primarily a competitor. Instead, they are finding myriad reasons to suggest that we are by nature cooperators—and that our position at the top of the evolutionary heap has come about precisely because of this innate ability and propensity to work together toward a common good. Our greatest survival tool is not the club or the knife or the ability to harness fire. Our greatest tool is language—the instrument that allows us to take the giant step beyond "me first" competition to "good for us all" cooperation.

If this is true (and I believe it is), then we make a terrible mistake in teaching our young that they must be winners *no matter what*, and that they ought to be perfect. In teaching the first, we are going against the grain of our true nature. In teaching the second, we are preparing them only for disillusionment.

Other cultures have understood these things better than we have. In certain primitive societies, there is no word in the language for "me." And in the culture that preceded ours here in northern Minnesota, a charming and valuable custom kept perfection in its rightful place.

For here, among the Ojibwe, it was the custom of bead workers to deliberately misplace a single bead in any given piece of work. That bead was called the humility bead, and it reminded all who saw it that perfection belonged only to the Great Spirit, and was not a quality given to humankind.

Narrative

Following several months of fruitless search through the area around Bemidji, I had a long talk with my oldest friend, Bill Walker, who also hailed from Illinois and had attended St. Olaf. He suggested we join forces and look for land together. In the spring of '65 we found a place that fit the bill: 40 acres spanning the outlet creek of a lake northeast of Pine River and boasting a tumbledown 12x20-foot shack. Asking price: $2,000. We ruthlessly whittled the price down to $1950, arranged a contract for deed, and, in early May, took possession of the property.

Later that same month I met Claire Ringdahl, my wife-to-be. Aware that summer in the north woods was notoriously short, I commenced digging the foundations for a small house, using a borrowed shovel, and helped Bill drive a shallow well topped by a hand pump. Luckily the land was mostly sand. Claire's dad, a carpenter, helped frame the deck and walls. In August, overlooking Hand Lake before an altar of birch and split pine, he gave his daughter's hand to me in marriage. The assembled guests, standing on a carpet of pine needles or seated on lawn chairs, clapped lustily when the minister gave his blessing. Already the woods had worked its magic, doing away with the need for an elaborate indoor ceremony and other fancy—and expensive—rituals.

Fall came wetly that year, slowing our work on the little house. At night I wrote children's stories and sent them off to market, and each day we walked to the mailbox with held breath, hoping there'd be a check inside. Sometimes there was—usually for $20 or $25. Claire established a food budget of $10 per week, augmented by fish caught from the creek. The local lumber yard grew uneasy as our bill for building materials mounted, but somehow we managed to get them something each month, and in early November we moved out of the drafty old shack and into our newly insulated house. We had no indoor plumbing, wall paneling, or floor covering; that would come later. In the meantime, we were warm.

In 1965, in the woods of north-central Minnesota, life was still lived close to the bone. Insurance was something reserved for the well-to-do. Several of our neighbors had hand pumps that stuck up through the linoleum of their kitchen countertops and drained into a single-compartment sink and, from there, out into a buried 55-gallon drum. Toilets were located out back. Heating was done via wood in a Warm Morning stove. The summer's produce was kept in an outdoor root cellar.

Refrigeration for many (including us) meant a wooden-clad icebox stocked once a week with a 75-pound block of ice. We bought the ice from a neighbor who sawed it out of a nearby pond and kept it in a double-walled log icehouse, insulated with several tons of sawdust. We found ice tongs at a garage sale for 50 cents and hauled the blocks in the trunk of our car, just like everybody else.

During the fall we took baths at the outdoor well, splashing the icy water against each other with demonic glee. Come winter, we resorted to sponge baths with water heated over the stove. For the first time in our lives, we learned to appreciate warm running water—an appreciation gained only by its absence.

We learned that our neighbors disliked leaving their homesteads in order to make money. "Working out," they called it—and kept it to a minimum. Far better to plant a big garden, shoot a deer or two, spear washtubs of northerns and walleyes during the spring spawning runs, keep a flock of laying hens, maybe fatten a pig or a heifer, and supplement the whole enterprise with a few hundred pounds of wild rice. "Ricin'," it turned out, was hard work. Poling a makeshift rice boat or canoe through miles of resistant reeds was not a job for the undermuscled. Nor was the picker's task easy. You knelt on a cushion and bent the stalks of rice over the thwart with one stick and tapped the ripe kernels off the stalks with another, ignoring the pain in your cramped legs, the itch of rice hulls that got down your shirt, and the jitter and jiggle of thousands of bugs.

Gone Ricin'

"What do you think?"

"Bear to the right. It's thicker there."

I ease the paddle into the water and the canoe glides to the right. Another stroke and the *skreaking* begins; the unforgettable sound of wild rice stalks scraping against the aluminum hull of the canoe.

My wife, Claire, sitting before me and half-hidden beneath a floppy straw hat, reaches out with her right hand, in which she holds a feather-light cedar stick. She pulls a sheaf of stalks toward the canoe, bends it gently over the gunwale, and taps it with the stick in her other hand. A shower of rice kernels spatters into the canoe. She releases the stalks and they spring back upright, some of them still festooned with rice that's not quite ripe. Harvesting wild rice is a delicate business. If you're patient, there'll be more to get another day.

We work our way through the green-gold forest, the top of which stands a yard or more above the canoe. Sunshine spangles the occasional patch of open water. Sora rails spring skyward ahead of us, launching themselves like little helicopters, their tiny legs hanging rearward as they fly. We hear the sudden *whop-whop-whop* of wood ducks taking flight and watch as they arrow ahead a few hundred yards and then settle back on the water.

A trickle of sweat worms its way down my back as I switch the paddle from one side to the other. We're into the rhythm now, rice sticks swinging from right to left, right to left, then left to right, left to right. I propel us forward at a steady crawl. Out here on the rice bog, patience pays.

A frog dives off its lily-pad raft, perturbed by our intrusion. Spiders fall through the golden air and land on the growing cushion of rice on the floor of the canoe. A thousand little flea-like bugs do acrobatics above the mound of rice. I close my eyes and savor the sounds; the *skreak* of stalks, the patter of rice, the clack of sticks, the burble of water against the hull.

The sun beats down upon our necks. When we come to an open patch of water, we rest. Claire leans to the side so I can see our haul. The mound of rice looks fuzzy, in need of a shave. She plucks a kernel from the pile and shows me the hair that protrudes from one end. The jiggle of movement has tipped the hairs upright, causing a beard to form.

Later, heading back toward shore through lengthening shadows, we marvel together at the way the blues and pinks of the sky merge with the surface of the lake. If it's true that the word "Minnesota" means the land of sky-tinted waters, our state has been aptly named. Nowhere is this clearer than on a wild rice pond.

By the time we beach the canoe, we've had enough for one day. We transfer our harvest onto a blanket, ball it up, and hoist it into the trunk of the car. A skein of mallards winds above the far shore, outlined against the setting sun. The air is already cooler and gives promise of a pleasant night's sleep. We stuff the paddles and rice sticks under the thwarts, push the cushions under the seat, and turn the canoe upside down.

"Glad we came?" I ask, as we walk back to the car.

Claire smiles. "You betcha."

September Song

There's something about a grey September day that makes the heart grow melancholy.

Shakespeare, in his sonnet No. 73, captures this brooding sense of autumn when he likens himself to the season.

"That time of year thou mayest in me behold
When yellow leaves, or none, or few, do hang
Upon those boughs which shake against the cold,
Bare ruin'd choirs where late the sweet birds sang."

There is, with the dying of the leaves and the departure of the birds, a literal loss. Summer is gone; mere memories remain. The choir lofts where late the sweet birds sang are empty now, but the sight of them recalls the loveliness of the songs, and the very beauty that enthralled us earlier in the year now causes sadness.

For it is fall, the antithesis of spring, a time of letting go. Things fall in fall; leaves, fruits, temperatures, sap, spirits. The springing up which happened half a year ago must now subside. Plants and animals prepare to rest. The soil has earned a respite, too. The great cycle of life curves down and in.

As the preacher of the Old Testament assures us, "for every thing there is a season, and a time for every matter under heaven; a time to be born, and a time to die; a time to plant, and a time to pluck up what is planted."

Where, then, does the melancholy come from?

From the joy. Where else?

But how easily we forget its source, how quick we are to feel cast out, forlorn. And how readily we try to distract ourselves, to numb our hearts against the sorrow.

I think this is a bad mistake.

Kahlil Gibran, in *The Prophet*, wrote: "The deeper that sorrow carves into your being, the more joy you can contain." By distracting ourselves we avoid the growth that, eventually, allows us to feel greater happiness. The truth of the matter is not that joy is greater than sorrow, nor sorrow greater than joy, but that they are inseparable.

So when the leaves flutter earthward and the frost turns the flowers grey, it's proper to feel downhearted. That is, perhaps, September's function: to prepare us for the greater losses; the loss of youth, the loss of loved ones, the loss of life itself. The challenge is to celebrate that which we value, and then to muster the grace and dignity to let it go.

As Shakespeare's sonnet concludes,

"This thou perceiv'st, which makes thy love more strong,
To love that well which thou must leave ere long."

Narrative

That first winter we learned several lessons the hard way. One evening I left the handle of the outdoor pump in the wrong position. The next morning the pump was no longer useable, its body ruptured by expanding ice, so we had to take our water from the creek. A spur-of-the-moment decision to drive down an unplowed back road left us stranded for half a day. Lacking an engine block heater, battery charger, or garage, we found our car unstartable during severe cold spells. I tried to find work as a carpenter and, desperate, agreed to frame in a cabin for a dollar an hour, only to be replaced by two even more desperate fellows who charged 50 cents. At the end of January, broke and frustrated, we accepted Claire's parents' offer to come live with them for the balance of winter. A borrowed $100 allowed us to drive to Seattle, where we quickly found jobs and began to replenish our coffers.

In spring, we returned to the woods, planted a garden, and resumed work on the house. Little by little we were learning how to make do. We bought an old treadle-powered sewing machine and Claire began patching our clothes and creating some new ones. An investment in Mason jars and a used pressure cooker allowed us to can the garden produce. I learned the rudiments of masonry from an experienced friend who built us a beautiful stone fireplace, and that fall I undertook building one for hire; the first of several hundred constructed over the ensuing 40 years.

Packets of Life

I magine, if you can, a time capsule wherein life could be packaged up and kept on hold for as long as you wanted, free from the wear and tear that normally assails it. You'd label the package, put it on the shelf, and wait till conditions were just right. Then you'd open it, add some water, and presto! Life would spring forth, wriggling its ancient toes down into the earth and lifting its fingers toward the sun.

Sound far-fetched?

It isn't. Astonishing as it might seem, such mechanisms already exist, and have for millions of years. They're common as raindrops and just as beneficial. We call them seeds.

Because they're such an everyday part of our experience, we tend to take them for granted. But each contains the extraordinary ability to transcend time.

Using this ingenious device, Nature takes the DNA of the parent, puts it into safekeeping, and holds it for as long as necessary for it to find a propitious chance at a new life. While it's true that most seeds gradually lose their viability over time, there are instances of that time stretching on a long way—lotus seeds taken from a peat bog in Manchuria and radiocarbon dated at a thousand years old were coaxed into producing flowering plants.

Given the advances in cryogenic technology—the ability to freeze-dry organisms and keep them intact for decades—some people now elect to have their dead bodies frozen in the hope that some day they may be resuscitated and given another chance to live. But this is a cumbersome and expensive process, and one not likely to succeed. Even if it did, the resurrected body would be as old and worn as it was at the time of its original death.

Seeds, on the other hand, allow life to be put on hold for a generation or two and then resumed with a minimum of fuss and bother. They permit the life force to lie dormant for as long as convenient or necessary, and then to continue within a brand-new body. In this sense they defy the normal ravages of time.

Knowing this, you have to wonder what, exactly, triggers a seed to return to life. We commonly regard water and sunlight as the elements necessary for germination; but in a way that begs the question. Might there be some guiding awareness in the seed itself that senses when conditions are right, when the moisture and heat levels are such that germination can succeed? Is this a purely mechanical activity at the molecular level, or is there some sort of intelligence involved? In the wild, under drought conditions, many grasses "elect" not to grow for a year, either lying dormant or extending their root systems while waiting for atmospheric circumstances to improve.

The marvelous design of seeds allows them movement in space as well as time. Because they're tiny and light in weight, they can be distributed over long distances by wind and water, by hitching a ride on the fur or feathers of animals and birds, or by being eaten and eliminated by them. The expulsion systems that some fruits have developed shoot them several feet away from the mother plant.

We tend to regard seeds as humdrum but, in fact, they border on the miraculous, and without them we couldn't exist. Next time you're ready to plant some, take a moment to study them and give thanks.

Seeds—the incredible, elegant packets of life.

A Walk on the Wild Side

A week ago last Sunday my wife and I went for a walk on the wild side. Not a long walk, really; a half-mile or so each way. But it was on the wild side, along an old sand road unsullied by herbicides or the slash of the highwayman's sickle.

Luckily, my wife does not suffer from my near-total ignorance when it comes to identifying wildflowers. Even more luckily, she is very diplomatic when it comes to sharing information.

"Look, Honey," she said as we started on our walk. "Isn't the fireweed beautiful?"

I followed her pointing finger toward a cluster of spiky pink flowers and murmured agreement. "And look at the vetch," she continued, directing my gaze downward toward what looked amazingly similar to a pea patch. We stopped and bent down toward the purplish-blue flowers and felt of the miniature pods.

A little while later we came to a chokecherry tree and examined the still-green clusters of cherries. Not too many weeks till they would turn nearly black and end up in a jar of jelly. I could almost taste them spread thick on a slice of toast.

"Hey, " I cried. "Wild geraniums." At last—a flower whose name I remembered.

"Very good," said my wife, encouraging me as a good teacher should. "And look at those little yellow flowers each growing at the tip of a stalk of grass. Those are one of my favorites—yellow-eyed grass."

And so we proceeded, moving leisurely down the road, learning and marveling and seeing an incredible variety of ordinary things that somehow no longer seemed ordinary.

Within a mere ten yards we saw fresh deer tracks, two agates, a rabbit, several clusters of green acorns, a profusion of little pinkish bell-shaped flowers on a shrub called dogbane, and helped ourselves to a smattering of ripe wild raspberries.

A little later I learned that a delicate yellow five-petaled flower was called cinquefoil (from the French words for five leaves), that a white bulb-shaped flower bore the apt but somewhat off-putting name of bladder campion, that another white flower was known as hoary alyssum, and still another (this one with feathery leaves) was called yarrow.

"Jeez," I said as we walked along, "there sure is a lot to learn."

"Here," said my wife, "have a Juneberry." We munched on the purple berries and wished there were enough to make a pie. Then we turned around and started back—and the marvels didn't cease.

We passed bunches of fresh hazelnuts and clumps of pin cherries glowing like miniature red lights and bent to see the fragile beauty of wild blackberry flowers, their white petals peppered with minute black dots.

Toward the end we paused to admire the seed ball of a goatsbeard plant, which looks exactly like a giant dandelion gone to pieces, and later we watched an ant struggling to move a dead moth twenty times its size.

The next day, Monday, I drove down the same road intent on getting to work and didn't see a thing.

Blessed October

No month compares with October.

October is one-of-a-kind, an experience, an offbeat step in the otherwise orderly march of the year.

September is often in the rain. November is a down-to-business month, bringing the certain news of winter.

But October, blessed October...

It's at once a state of grace, a trickster, and a passion. One's blood runs to wine in October. Forgotten springtime fantasies swirl back into the brain, turning one giddy with gladness. There is such promise in this month, such beauty, such lusty purity.

Never is the sky bluer than during October. Never are the colors more provocative, the air so spanking clean. Spring is the time of endlessness, the teenhood of the year. Autumn is life after 40. In October you know the year is mortal. You know that death will come. And knowing that, you sense a piquancy, a special tang. October is life after the first hard frost; the heart attack that you survived.

The spiraling leaves remind you of loved ones gone before. The migrating birds are like your own children leaving home. You feel both wistful and somehow relieved. There is a sadness in the air, and mixed together with it is a joy so overarching and supreme it leaves you breathless.

For you know that next year—with you or without you—the cycle will come round again, and birds will return, and days will grow longer, and green plants will stretch upward toward the sun. In the meantime you are freed from cutting grass and weeding gardens and swatting mosquitoes and tending to the needs of summer visitors.

October is a time of fullness; a harvest moon; a chance to put aside worry and fear.

The wise person takes pleasure in this month.

October is an affirmation and a gift.

Narrative

In November of 1966, just as we preparing to settle in for the winter, I was drafted into the U.S. Army and ordered to report for active duty the day after Christmas. Following much anguished discussion, we decided the best bet was for Claire to move down to Illinois and live with my folks for the duration. The Vietnam War was raging and it looked as though I'd become part of it. But after stateside training, I was shipped to Germany, and served my time fighting the sitzkrieg. Claire flew over to join me for the final six months, and we found a tiny apartment in the Schwabian village of Eschenbach, bought a $200 VW beetle, and set about exploring southern Germany on weekends.

Room in the Inn

I n the waning days of 1967 I was a young G.I. stationed in southern Germany. Thanksgiving had come and gone and now Christmas loomed ahead. It promised to be a singularly unmerry event. I was homesick as hell and most of the people I held dear lived on the far side of the Atlantic Ocean.

Then the postcard came.

"Meet me in St. Moritz for Christmas. We can celebrate by skiing. Bring friends. Hanno."

Hanno was my former college German teacher, living in Germany during his sabbatical year. My spirits began soaring toward the height of the legendary Swiss Alps to which the postcard beckoned. No matter that I was a novice skier. Suddenly the world had regained its luster.

Early on Saturday morning, a few days before Christmas, my roommate Tom and I and our mutual buddy Mike headed south in Mike's VW bus. All the way to the border the sky was heavily overcast, the sun a vague silver coin in the mist. Then as we crossed into Austria the clouds parted and sunshine filled the sky. "Good sign," said Mike. His words were to prove prophetic.

We drove on through the day, across the neck of Austria and through the tiny principality of Liechtenstein, on into Switzerland and the famous Alps. Night fell and on we drove, finally reaching St. Moritz around ten. After some confusion we found the address Hanno had given, which proved to be a half-timbered villa overlooking a lake. I knocked upon the door, only to find there had been some mix-up, that Hanno was already on his way back to Germany, and that the villa was closed for the holidays.

A hasty tour of town confirmed what I had begun to suspect: we were up a Swiss creek without a paddle. St. Moritz was a playground for the well-to-do; it was almost Christmas; lodging was, to put it mildly, at a premium. Desperate, we returned to the villa and explained our plight. Please, we pleaded. We have no place to stay. Thus began a three-day fairy tale.

The proprietors of the villa, two elderly English spinsters, agreed to open their establishment to us. The next morning a knock on the door awoke us to the smell of hot chocolate and freshly baked rolls, served to us in bed. Later we drove downtown, marveling at the grandeur of the mountains rising up from the shores of the lake. We gawked at the cars parked along the streets: Ferraris, Aston Martins, Rolls Royces. A mere Mercedes was definitely downscale here.

We bought tickets and took an aerial cable car up over the lake to the top of the mountains and spent half a day in a stone-and-glass lodge sipping hot wine and watching the rich and famous ski. For supper we went to an elegant restaurant our hosts had recommended and ate stuffed veal cutlets so tender and tasty we thought we'd died and gone to gourmet heaven.

And on it went. Each morning the gentle tap at the door brought mouth-watering breakfasts, followed by high adventure all day long. On Christmas Eve our hosts insisted that we eat with them, and sent us down to the wine cellar to pick out several bottles of vintage grape. They served a dinner with so many courses we quit counting, and afterward we all sat around the fireplace sipping champagne and swapping stories. Just before midnight they had us throw open the huge casement windows so that we could hear the bells, layer after layer after layer of snow-gentled tolling, as sounds from every bell in Switzerland rolled majestically down the mountain valleys.

By the time we were ready to leave, we found ourselves nearly broke. Typical G.I. behavior—spend now, worry later. We decided we'd have to wire back to the base for money.

But when, after some stammering, we explained our plight, the spinsters just smiled and presented us with a basket full of food for our trip home.

"We'd already decided you don't owe us a thing," they said. "We refuse to accept any money. On the very first Christmas there was no room in the inn. We would never want that to happen again."

Narrative

Living in Europe taught us to celebrate diversity. Languages, dress, foods, buildings, social traditions—all varied from country to country and even from county to county. There was no such thing as one right way to skin the cat. A month before my time in the service was over, we took advantage of accumulated leave time and went on a three-week jaunt north, driving our little blue gas-sipper and camping in an Army pup tent. We worked our way up the Rhine, swung through the Low Countries, went half crazy with joy at seeing dozens of Rembrandts and Van Goghs in the Rijksmuseum in Amsterdam, spent a magical night on the Frisian island of Texel, continued up through Denmark (where we fell in love with Copenhagen), took the overnight car ferry to Norway, and spent an unforgettable week island-hopping up the coast to Bergen. By the time we returned to Germany, we were tempted to stay in Europe for the rest of our lives.

But the call of our little homestead proved stronger. In September of 1968 we flew back to the states, where I enrolled at Moorhead State College for the purpose of getting proper teaching credentials. Lots of late-night talks had convinced us we needed a regular income. We wanted to add on to the house, we needed a dependable car, and we both felt it was time to start a family. Nine months later and fully credentialed, I was hired to teach English and German at Pequot Lakes High School. And a few months after that our first child, Christopher, arrived.

Teaching turned out to be lots of work, and also lots of fun. My senior English students put together a literary magazine, started a weekly in-school TV program using a new-fangled device called a video camera, and began publishing an in-school newspaper called The Good Times. In the spring of 1970, the faculty got the students organized to celebrate the first Earth Day, during which the kids planted thousands of trees around the perimeter of the campus, cleaned up the city park and miles of roadsides, and successfully petitioned the city council to close the town dump, an open wound that was oozing pollutants into nearby Sibley Lake. I spent summers building fireplaces with my brother, Bill, sweating and grunting and generally enjoying the chance to rebuild sagging muscles. In late fall of 1971 our second child, a daughter named Kia, came to grace our lives.

Then, in the winter, I was approached by three friends who wanted to start a newspaper. Since none of them had any journalistic experience, they were seeking to hire someone who did. I told them I was just their man. I'd coedited the student weekly newspaper at college, overseen the establishment of various publications while teaching, and sold a couple hundred articles and stories to various minor venues through the years.

My enthusiasm had a secret dimension. I'd been working after hours on a novel. But this conflicted with the nightly chore of correcting several dozen school assignments. Maybe running a country weekly would allow sufficient free time for writing fiction.

Or maybe not. From the first issue of The Country Echo onward, I found myself working 80 to 100 hours a week, and continued at that pace for the next four years. It became clear that we couldn't afford to keep the printer we'd hired, so I let him go and taught myself how to run the offset press, which I did for more than a year. As with any new business, cash flow was a recurrent problem, necessitating frequent forays to the bank to plead for additional loans. In order to be closer to the office, we sold our home north of Pine River, moved an outbuilding onto acreage near Pequot Lakes, and hunkered down in rather primitive conditions, in essence duplicating the experience we'd endured several years earlier. To help advertise our services, I consented to do a daily radio show via telephone with a station out of Brainerd. The show was unrehearsed and tended toward the chaotic. But month after month more subscribers signed up to take our paper, and in 1976 we launched a second publication, The Echoland Shopper, which proved profitable from the very first issue. By that time, however, I was tired to the bone and wanted out. We put the business up for sale and waited for a buyer. The first one who came along insisted I stay on board to manage it for an additional year. At the end of that time, he sold it to a second buyer and I agreed to stay around for a final six months. Finally it was sold to Keith and Martha Anderson, under whose devoted guidance it grew to maturity. In 1981, as mentioned in the preface, they suggested I start writing a biweekly column and gave me a free hand as to subject matter. From the beginning, I tried to make the essays reader-friendly and homespun, and chose to avoid topics of a deliberately political nature on the theory that, like sleeping dogs or poisonous snakes, some subjects are best left undisturbed.

After selling the Echo, I devoted most of the next few winters to writing fiction and spent the summer months relaxing with Claire and the kids. Together we managed to make up for some of the time I'd been absent running the newspaper. We played baseball, went swimming and fishing, built forts, went for long walks, and expanded the garden. We acquired a flock of laying hens, took several trips, and remodeled the house. When the money from the sale of the paper ran out, I spent a winter horse logging with my lifelong friend Bill Walker, cutting firewood off a Potlatch permit and skidding the logs with Bill's big Belgian mare named Maude. In the spring, I resumed doing stonework and found the vigorous physical work refreshing.

Life Says Yes

As one who long ago developed the unfortunate habit of watching the evening news, I find it hard at times to keep on smiling. So much of what invades the living room is negative, so much insane, that all the good things seem shrunken before the relentless litany of bad.

But now I have an antidote to gloom.

When the news of the day begins to curl my lip, I simply turn the TV off and saunter on out to the chicken coop.

There, spread before me on a mat of tangled straw, I see the good news—baby chicks tottering about on two-day-old legs, following their mothers as they learn about the mysteries of food and drink, cheeping for all they are worth.

Here, in the midst of molted feathers and old barn smells, I find the haven that modern life does not provide. For here I see the ritual drama of ongoing life, staged not for profit or Nielsen ratings, blessedly free from commercials. Here in the barn life is real, unaffected. Here I see life saying yes.

For three weeks the hens sat patiently upon the eggs, getting off only for a bit of feed and some water. Day and night, Sphinx-like, they peered up at us from their duties, clucking when we got too close, obeying the instinctive command to warm and protect the eggs.

And then, two days ago, we heard the first new cry of life, a muffled cheeping from beneath the hen on the middle nest. Hours later, we watched as a downy yellow head appeared and a pair of brand-new eyes took a first look at the world.

The next day there were three new chicks. One, just hatched, fell out of the nest and appeared to be dead. My wife brought it into the house and put it under a lamp. A few hours later it too began to cheep. By nightfall it was back beneath its mother and doing just fine.

Now there are five, with the promise of several more to come. We watch, fascinated, as the little fluff balls toddle to the feeder and imitate the actions of their elders. And we smile with delight when they move to the waterer, where they dip their tiny beaks into the tray and then tilt their heads up high so the water will slide down their throats.

Together with the greening grass and budding trees, our pint-size flock of newborn chicks reminds us of the rightness of things, and tells us eloquently what the TV cannot—that life is a thundering *yes*, ancient and ongoing, a mysterious, marvelous gift.

A Benediction

We saw the coyote before it saw us.

The four of us were coming around the corner where our sand driveway meets the township road and suddenly there it was, trotting ahead of us on the road, its bushy tail pluming out behind it in a silken grace of movement. As if prearranged, we stopped and held our breath.

The coyote sensed our presence. With a casual flick of its head the amber eyes swung back to take us in. The trot became a lope, the tail held lower now, and we watched without a word as it sped away, its movement so liquid and smooth as to leave us half-mesmerized. With a sudden turn and a long arching leap it left the road and gained the woods.

We moved ahead, our eyes on the trees, until we were abreast of where it had turned off the road. Then, to our great delight, we saw it again. It stood on a low hill some fifteen yards away, watching us. The angle of view revealed its creamy undersides and elegant proportion of legs to body. Again we stood transfixed, willing it to stay. But it had business of its own, and moments later turned away and sauntered out of sight into the underbrush.

As soon as it was gone, we all began to talk at once. We chattered on, congratulating one another on our great good luck. Then we turned to retrace the paw prints in the soft sand road, as if to reassure ourselves that what we had seen was no mirage.

When we got home, we did a little checking in the books.

The coyote breeding season starts in January and lasts through February. There is substantial evidence that coyotes pair for life. After breeding, the female seeks a den site and prepares the den for birthing.

The gestation period lasts 58 to 63 days, which means the pups are generally born in April. The litter averages from five to seven pups, born blind and helpless and covered with brownish-gray woolly fur. When the pups are newborn, the male often assists by bringing food to the female. Later he may bring food that the female tears into pieces for the pups.

The pups venture from the den for the first time at three weeks, but do not stay out for very long until they are six or seven weeks old. The pups are weaned at eight weeks, at which time the female teaches them to hunt. A month or so later the pups leave the den area and disperse to form territories of their own. Usually they don't mate until two years of age. Adult females average 25 pounds, males 30.

The coyote is not loved by all. But increasing research has disproved many popular misconceptions, showing for example that coyote predation is not a serious cause of overall deer mortality, and that farmers who practice good husbandry by penning their stock at night and properly disposing of dead animals have few predation problems.

In any event, the coyote (or brush wolf, as it is often called) occupies an important niche in the natural scheme. And for those of us fortunate enough to chance upon one in the wild, there is a special feeling of benediction. In its presence we sense the magnificence and the diversity of life's many forms, and are reminded of our common heritage as fellow riders on the earth.

The February Garden

All good gardens start in February.

This phase of horticulture is not only the cheapest and least strenuous, but also the grandest, in that one's dreams may grow toward greatness, unfettered by such paltry things as crabgrass or an insufficiency of fertilizer.

In the garden of one's February dreams, the cabbages grow green as dollar bills and round as basketballs, undefiled by moth or worm. The cornstalks stretch to stately heights, each stalk the bearer of a perfect golden ear, not one of which is ravaged by raccoons. The tomato plants resemble Christmas trees, festooned with bright red ornaments, and like the tannenbaum they are immune to frost.

In the February garden there are no rabbits, no ravens, no aphids, no deer. No squash bugs, no gophers, no borers, no blight. This is a place unacquainted with potassium deficiency and drought. No hail falls here. Damaging winds are deflected by a shield of dreams. It is a place uncorrupted, a Garden of Eden, untainted by insecticides or grief. At its edge in the shade of a rose-covered trellis, the gardener may sit all day long, able to work his or her green-thumb magic without having to lift a finger. For in this garden neither sweat doth drip, nor blister form, nor pain assault the lower back, nor stiffness seize the joint.

All plants flourish in the February garden, attaining a fullness and luster otherwise seen only in seed catalogs. Succulence is the norm. Merely by closing one's eyes can one taste the sweet nectar of ripe muskmelons, sniff the tang of white onions, feel the crunch of fresh carrots between the teeth.

Things grow to maturity here. Beets attain the size of softballs. Broccoli plants rival small trees. The loving gardener leaves a pumpkin for the kids to hollow out so they will have a fort in which to play.

And best of all, the produce finds its own way into Mason jar and freezer bag. The green beans snap themselves into uniform lengths, all ready for consumption. The cucumbers grab a garland of dill before slicing themselves into pickles. The squash leap unaided into the attic; the potatoes spring willingly into their burlap sacks. Thus are February gardeners spared distraction, so that they may devote full attention to the sketching of plans and the scribbling of lists, confident that dirty fingers will not soil the paper, serene in the knowledge that the weeds of reality will not encroach upon their dreams.

The Great Gift of Dirt

For those who live here in the northland, there is no season as splendid as spring. The melting of the snow, the reappearance of the soil, the returning of the birds, the budding of the trees—all are occasions worthy of fervent celebration. In a wiser civilization, there would, I think, be special times set aside for the observance of these wonders. Melting Day, say, or Greening Week, or Migration Month. Children would be let out of school and adults would be given leave of absence from their work and everybody would go delirious with spring fever.

Until we gain a truer vision of what matters, we'll have to content ourselves with celebrating this ancient miracle of renewal as best we can.

For starters we can pick up a handful of earth and hold it and smell it and taste it and ponder the fact that without the soil we wouldn't be here. This dirt is the womb and the cradle, the bed and the casket of all life forms.

Eons ago the earth was one mass of rock and the only living things were microbes. These single-celled bacteria and fungi liberated carbon dioxide and acids, thereby beginning the process of breaking rock down into soil. Later lichens and mosses began to cover the exposed rock, slowly forming a film of material that provided a foothold for the plants and trees that succeeded them. These processes, together with the climatic effects of heat and cold, wind and rain, and the pulverizing power of glaciers, account for the most overlooked treasure on the planet: the great gift of dirt.

We denigrate this material daily, and as a nation we treat it with contempt. It takes nature several hundred years to make one inch of topsoil. In the few centuries that North Americans have farmed this continent, an estimated 60 percent of its topsoil has been destroyed.

We grow from infancy learning to devalue the ground of our existence. We are taught to think negatively about anything "dirty" or "dirt cheap" or "soiled," when in fact there is no resource even remotely as complex and valuable as dirt.

The great majority of all life forms live in the top few inches of the earth's surface, and it is this same thin blanket of beneficence that recycles all creatures back into the elements from which they came, permitting them to spring up again into new packages of life, to dance their little while upon the planet until they, too, return into the ever-renewing earth.

When we dig a hole or hoe a garden or stand in mourning at a grave, we are in the presence of the sacred, the sublime.

The deepest and most magnificent mysteries lie not out there beyond the stars, but right here underfoot.

Turtle Eggs

For the past many years our family has lived at the end of a long sand road. Muddy in spring, dusty in summer, prone to develop potholes and vulnerable to encroaching weeds, our unpaved drive requires more upkeep than its asphalted cousins.

But the inconvenience fades to insignificance when the turtles come to lay their eggs. From late May to mid-June our sand road becomes a half-mile-long incubator of reptiles, and we feel strange stirrings of pride and anxiety, parental at root.

Not all the turtles choose to deposit their eggs in the roadway. Some we find laboring up near the garden, others over by the shed. But there is something about that open stretch of sand that the majority of turtles find inviting, and it is generally near the edge of the road that the nests themselves are placed.

It takes time to watch a turtle dig—and the watching is rewarded. There is something so ancient and reassuring about a turtle digging a hole that your cares and preoccupations seem to diminish with each whisk of the creature's hind feet.

I have tried to measure the amount of earth a turtle moves per stroke, but find the calculation inexact. A third of a thimbleful? Not much, for sure. But turtles are noted for perseverance, and in time the hole grows large enough so that the digger is tilted clearly toward the rear, like a customized car of the '50s.

When the hole is judged large enough, the female deposits her clutch of eggs and commences to cover them back up. Then she lumbers back toward the marsh and leaves the worrying to us.

Fortunately, each year my wife and I seem less able to remember things with great precision. After a rainfall or two, the exact location of the eggs is lost to all but the inhabitants thereof, and we don't have to fret about whether we are crushing a new generation of turtles when we swerve the car to avoid hitting a rabbit.

Unfortunately, there are some other creatures sharing our homestead who have better memories and different tastes than we do. Skunks, raccoons, snakes, even the family dog—all have been suspected of visiting the underground nursery with intent not to nurture but to ingest.

We take solace in reminding ourselves about the Great Chain of Being, and have found through the years that the turtle population hereabouts seems to be holding its own.

Each spring the precious spark of life is passed along, ensuring the endurance of this strange and plodding creature with the house upon its back. And we who are lucky enough to live at the end of sand roads are blessed with the chance to witness yet another of nature's miracles.

Huck and the Kids

Sitting in the screen porch the other night, sipping a drink and listening to the ancient sound of loons calling back and forth on the lake, I got to remembering the summer of The Book.

Our son, Chris, was ten or eleven that year, our daughter, Kia, two years younger, and their dear friend, Billy, came up from southern Minnesota to spend a week with us. For kids that age summer lasts forever, and the prospect of tramping in the woods and going fishing and swimming and sitting around a campfire filled them all with boundless excitement.

But what turned that week into the stuff of legend was a book. The book was written by a fellow using the alias of Mark Twain, and was titled *The Adventures of Huckleberry Finn*.

Each night, long after supper was over and the last hint of twilight had faded into darkness, the kids and I would assemble in the screened porch, fire up an old kerosene lantern, wriggle into comfortable positions, and commence hanging out with Huck. A few sentences into each night's installment the years would drop away and, instead of the distant drone of traffic on the highway, we'd hear the mournful whistle of a steamboat on the Mississippi and feel the prickle of excitement as Huck crept through the shadows into a new predicament.

We joined him as he sneaked out of the Widow Douglas's house at night to rendezvous with the Tom Sawyer gang; felt our scalps tighten with fear when Pap, his drunken father, forced him to drop out of school and kept him captive in a run-down shack in the woods; cheered mightily when he staged his own mock murder and escaped onto the river in a drifting canoe; felt waves of worry and joy as he joined Miss Watson's runaway slave, Jim, to begin their long and winding journey toward freedom on a raft.

Night after night we sat in the wavering circle of the lantern's yellow light and slipped back in time, hypnotized by the cadence of the sentences, citizens of a different world. From the darkness beyond the screens came the night sounds of owls hooing to and fro, of frogs croaking in the swamp, the distant *peent* of woodcocks and the faraway cry of whippoorwills.

Each time I stopped reading and looked up I'd see the yellow-orange cast of light on the kids' faces as, big-eyed, they imagined themselves on the Mississippi with Huck and Jim, while behind them, in the darkness, fireflies blinked their secret codes and starlight speckled the black sky.

I wanted to tell them how important the book is, and how many knowledgeable critics regard it as the best American novel ever written, but thankfully I held my tongue and let the story speak for itself. As it turned out, we never made it to the delicious encounter with the Duke of Bilgewater and the wandering, exiled Dauphin or the dreadful Arkansaw Difficulty; we simply ran out of time. But that's all right. What mattered was the experience, getting a taste of the magic.

Those nights occurred a long time ago, and have since alchemized into the stuff of dreams. Like Huck Finn, they've been transformed into the bright flame of something larger and more lasting than life itself; something clear and vivid, like the glow of the lantern and the luminous faces of the children watching from the shadows.

Narrative

Throughout the '80s, we worked at improving our homestead. Using wood we cut off the land, we built a sauna, expanded the house, and constructed a large shed to house a hydraulic stone splitter. The splitter provided work during inclement weather and allowed us to begin selling surplus stone to other area masons. We built a small but proper barn to house our growing flock of chickens and considered buying a milk cow. The kids were growing toward adolescence and consuming lots of food. In the end, we decided against getting a cow. Instead we purchased a stone grinder for making flour and started buying wheat in 50-pound sacks. Each week Claire ground fresh flour and baked half a dozen loaves of bread, an event that we all came to treasure. Christopher began cutting firewood to sell, purchased a pickup truck and log skidder, and kept us supplied with fuel for the winter's heat. Kia worked summers at local restaurants, waiting tables and putting money aside for college. We got lucky at an auction and managed to buy a 16x32-foot swimming pool for next to nothing. We erected the pool on the hillside just below the sauna, connected the two with a deck, and commenced to delight in taking the plunge.

Finland's Gift

We started building the sauna back in July.

It's set in the woods on the hill behind our house, nestled in a grove of young pin cherry trees.

What we wanted was something primitive and basic, a place stripped of all unnecessaries, and yet well-built and properly functional. We spent a lot of evenings kicking ideas around, guided largely by the history, theory, and examples shown in *The International Handbook of Finnish Sauna*, which we got from the library.

Right off we learned some basic facts. The word "sauna" is pronounced "sow-(as in pig) na" and refers not to the activity itself, but to the building in which it takes place (one does not take a sauna—one goes to the sauna.) Furthermore, the basic purpose of the sauna is to induce perspiration and thus to cleanse the skin and the body. It can be regarded as a bath but, since it cleanses the pores of the skin, removes impurities from the body, and forces the mind to relax, it does far more for the bather than the white shiny thing we call a tub.

The sauna has been used by the Finns for at least two thousand years. The facts that life involved very hard physical work and that timber, the raw material for building and fuel, was readily at hand, may explain the development of the sauna as a means both to cleanliness and renewed strength.

By all accounts, the sauna has always been a vital part of Finnish life. In the old days, children were born in the sauna, the bride visited the sauna before she went to the altar, and the aged were carried there to die. As it was the hottest room in a cold, damp climate, it served as a multipurpose kiln for the curing of meat and the drying of malt, hemp, flax, and other farm produce.

Many superstitions are connected with the sauna. The ancient Finns believed that fire came from heaven and was therefore sacred. For this reason, they looked upon the sauna as a holy place. Some people believe the practice of throwing water over the heated stones evolved as a form of sacrificial ceremony. The Finnish word *loyly* (the steam which rises from the stones) originally signified "spirit" or even "life," and a corresponding word in languages related to Finnish is *lil*, which means "soul."

The more we read, the more fascinated we became with both the design of the sauna and the extensive role it could play in one's life. No mere bathhouse, this. When we finally set to building, a hundred questions remained unresolved—but the calendar insisted we get started.

We used wood milled from our own land; tamarack and pine for the framing and paneling, aspen for the benches and duckboards. We chose to avoid electric light, and opted instead for candles. Since our sauna is not on the shore of a lake, washing will be via garden hose in the summer and snow banks in winter. (We haven't yet solved the problem of what to do in early spring and late fall.) The *Handbook* reminded us to cut plenty of birch branches while the leaves were still green, and put them in the freezer for use as winter *vihta* or whisks. My brother, Bill, consented to weld us up a stove, and we've got plenty of stones to place on top of it.

Now all that remains is to finish building the benches and doors, and hope that winter will bring with it plenty of nice fluffy snow. As soon as that happens, we'll trudge up the path and start enjoying Finland's gift to mankind.

The Chicks in the Mail

L ast week our family partook of an experience that linked us most satisfyingly with days gone by: we received a box of baby chickens in the U.S. Mail.

We ordered them from Sears, just like rural folks did over much of the past century. We purchased 50 of the little hummers, Rhode Island Reds, as hatched (which in theory gives you half males and half females), postpaid.

Prior to their arrival, we moved the laying hens to a new corner of the barn and remodeled their former quarters into something of a nursery, replete with low-hanging lights and a miniature feeding trough. We built a four-by-four-foot enclosure to keep the babies under the lights and carpeted the crib with sawdust from the shop. We laid in a big supply of chick starter so they'd have plenty to eat, and then we sat around biting our fingernails and calling the post office every morning to see if they had come.

Finally, on Thursday, the post office called us. My wife drove into town and returned bearing a cardboard box with dozens of half-inch holes and a picture of a newly-hatched chick printed on top, along with the warning: "BABY CHICKS—MUST HAVE AIR." Judging from the racket, which emerged from the little holes, our new arrivals were not suffering from oxygen deprivation.

We carried the box into the barn, snipped the restraining wires, and lifted the lid. Everyone began babbling at once. Huddled in the carton were 50 little balls of bright yellow fluff, each with two tiny legs and pencil-point eyes, and the cacophony of peeps that emerged from the tiny flock was so shrill it hurt your ears.

One by one we lifted them out of the box and put them into their new home. Within minutes they were clustered together under the warmth of the lights, peeping and pushing against one another with such vigor it seemed the ones toward the middle would be crushed.

We filled the feeder with food and sprinkled some on the sawdust and soon the more adventurous chicks began pecking away like old pros. An hour later one wandered over to the waterer, dipped its dwarf beak into the drink, and lifted its head up to swallow. Then another came over, and another, and soon drinking became the order of the day.

Each day since, the chicks have added new skills to their rapidly growing repertoire, scratching the sawdust for feed and an occasional bug, stretching up to full height (four inches) and beating the air with their stubby wings, preening, chasing one another round and round inside the small enclosure. If you cough or make some sudden movement they grow instantly silent. If you tap your finger on the side of their crib they rush over to investigate. And if you come into the barn when the sunbeams are falling just right through the windows, you will see them basking in the warmth just like their elders enjoy doing.

They came to us by mail, ordered from a catalog. But they have made us think some long and grateful thoughts about the miracle of growth and learning, and brought us joy and fascination in ways that other mail-borne purchases could never do.

In Praise of Instinct

Each year I find myself paying more attention to things I used to take for granted, and at the same time losing interest in certain notions I once found fascinating.

There was a time, for instance, when I thought man's reasoning power was the greatest force in the universe. Now, whenever I hear someone tout the importance of the human mind, I feel embarrassed. Great minds, eh? Look around at the damage we've inflicted on the planet. Look around and weep.

On the other hand, there was a time when instinct seemed to me a thing of little value. So a mallard knows when to fly south, and where to fly to, and when to fly back north and how to build a nest and rear its young. No big deal! Filled as I was with the idea of man's preeminence, I was blind to a true miracle.

My dictionary defines instinct as 1) "a natural or inherent aptitude, impulse, or capacity," and 2) "a largely inheritable and unalterable tendency by an organism to make a complex and specific response to environmental stimuli without involving reason and for the purpose of removing somatic tension." (Somatic is further defined as "of, relating to, or affecting the body, especially as distinguished from the germ plasm or the psyche.")

In other words, instinct is supposed to be some sort of automatic, built-in guidance system, inherited at birth and pretty much unchangeable, that tells an organism what to do and how to live. It's Mother Nature's software, inserted genetically into the embryo like a program popped into a computer.

If this is true, it strikes me as being nothing short of miraculous!

Imagine trying to write a Life Program for a mallard or a muskrat. To be successful (and all of Mother N's programs are successful, or her creatures would die off), you would have to include every conceivable scrap of information about migration and navigation, feeding and nutrition, site selection and nest-building design and construction techniques, dating and mating protocol, a seasonally fine-tuned birthing schedule, instructions about all aspects of nurturing the young, a predator recognition-and-avoidance system, etc., etc., etc.

Not only would you have to assemble and arrange this staggering sum of information, but you would have to encode it into the genes in such a way that it would be transmitted intact to each succeeding generation, a task approximately similar to engraving the entire text of several sets of encyclopedias onto something much smaller than the head of a pin.

This awesome, life-securing arrangement known as instinct is the very thing we humans are so ready to dismiss as unimportant on the grounds that it is inferior to our vaunted ability to reason.

And having reasoned that we alone among all life forms are possessors of spirits or souls, we can't resist adding a final putdown to our definition of this miracle. It exists, we conclude, "for the purpose of removing somatic tension."

What arrogance!

A Nose for Glory

There's something about the waning days of summer that heightens and sharpens one's sense of smell.

Perhaps it's the movement of vegetables from the garden into the house. Maybe it's just that so many things are ripe. Or possibly it's something psychological: the dimly perceived and quickly suppressed awareness that the green months are nearing their end, soon to be followed by winter.

Whatever the reasons, this time of the year abounds with extraordinary odors.

The tang, for instance, of dill sprigs hanging in the woodshed to dry.

The salty smell of a fresh tomato, plucked from the vine and munched in the garden, complete with leaf-smell and trickle of juice down the chin.

The sweet-and-sour smell of bread-and-butter pickles being readied on the stovetop.

The clove-like scent of crabapples being rendered into jelly. The yeasty odor of fresh bread baking in the oven, soon to be combined with the jelly into a slice of pure ecstasy.

And the jungly fragrance of a just-sliced cantaloupe, glowing before you like a harvest moon.

A walk to the woodpile brings to your nostrils the he-man scent of fresh-split oak, smelling surprisingly like the sweat it took to split it. This is an animal area. The popple whiffs of urine. A chunk of birch, lying all summer on the ground, gives off the musky hint of males in rut.

But next to the woodpile the stacks of drying pine lumber cologne the air with their pitchy perfume, as if they had doused themselves in aftershave for their up-coming trip to the planing mill.

Everywhere you go, the homestead exudes a riot of odors.

The marsh gives off a fetid, algal smell. Here summer itself seems to be decomposing. But along the roadside, where we recently mowed, the fragrance of drying grass rises up from the ground in a blessing.

In the chicken yard, the pile of strawy manure has grown acrid and wrinkles the nose. Now and again clouds scud over and raindrops pelt the earth, and when they do the earth itself gives forth a wondrous, ancient aroma, a strange amalgam of swamp and leaf mold and majesty; and it is then, particularly, that having a nose seems the greatest glory of them all.

Northern Lights

Saturday night. Supper was over, the dishes cleared away. Time to go up the hill to the sauna to fire the stove.

"Be back in a couple of minutes," I said, shrugging into my coat.

I stepped outside, expecting darkness. Instead the sky was light. I looked up, saw what it was, and hurried back into the house.

"Quick," I yelled. "Northern lights. The whole sky's lighted up."

A few minutes later we all stood staring upward, oohing and aahing at the pulsating shimmers of light in the night sky. Above us, as if centered right over our house, an enormous formation of bluish-white rays hovered in the shape of a maple leaf, the tips of which pointed east, north, and west. We watched, necks bent backward, as the eerie light quivered and spread.

"Wow! Look over there, toward the horizon. It's turning to purple."

"And lavender. And red."

We watched until our necks hurt, then trooped back inside. I headed straight to the encyclopedia.

"Aurora borealis," I read, "also called northern lights, is a glowing or flickering natural light seen at night in the sky of the Northern Hemisphere. A similar light that occurs in the Southern Hemisphere is called aurora australis.

"Auroral displays occur when protons and electrons are shot from the sun, striking the earth's upper atmosphere. The earth's magnetic field directs the particles toward the magnetic poles. As the particles move, they collide with atmospheric particles and change their electrical charge. They glow much like the charged particles of a fluorescent tube."

Reading on, I found that most auroral displays take place about 70 miles above the earth's surface, and are sometimes several times that height. Some extend in an arc for hundreds of miles. Long thin rays form what we see as curtains of light. Green is the most frequently seen color, caused by atomic oxygen. The red colors are caused by molecular oxygen and nitrogen. The displays appear to be most frequent at the time of greatest sunspot activity.

Later, on the way up to the sauna, the once magnificent lights had lessened to a gentle glow. I started the fire and stepped back outside. Silence. The curl of wood smoke scented the northern night. My breath plumed, faintly visible in the cold air. Down below yellow light spilled from the windows of the house out onto the curving banks of snow. Above the northern lights hung like delicate lace put out to dry. Through them I could see the stars.

The Wood Yard

For the past several months our son Christopher has been cutting firewood on a county cutting permit.

Each day he brings home a truckload of wood that he then stacks in his wood yard, sorted by species. There are rows of birch and rows of oak, rows of aspen and ash and maple, even one of elm.

A walk through the wood yard makes a person feel very good indeed. The fragrances of the various species tantalize the nose; the textures and colors of the neatly stacked piles delight the eye; the presence of thousands of pieces of drying wood gives comfort against the prospect of snow and cold.

It's a good place to stand and reflect upon things. The orderly ranks of wood provoke a calmness and simplicity of spirit, much like the careful arrangement of a Japanese garden. In the wood yard, beauty and utility shake hands. Though it is a place of death, a cellulose cemetery, the dominant sense is that of life. This wood has been cut and placed here for a purpose. This is no random sort of thing.

Close inspection reveals a delightful array of activity going on within the piles of wood. Chipmunks dash nervously in and out of the shadowed crevices. A red squirrel sits upon a throne of oak and holds forth in a lordly manner. Shreds of birch bark bespeak a nest of field mice. Various bugs scurry up and down the perpendicular faces of the piles, intent upon their work. And there, graced with miniature beads of dew, a spider's suspension bridge links the shores of oak and aspen.

Our son's wood yard is a sanctuary and a workplace, a garden and a school.

Study the ends of the logs. Bend down and look closely at the growth rings. Each piece of wood contains the story of its life written in circular script.

This chunk of popple, for instance—see how the rings near the center are spaced far apart? Those must have been wonderful years, full of warmth and plenty of moisture, years when this tree grew with the wild vitality of youth.

And look here, a little distance out, how the rings wrap tight around each other. These were years of leanness, years of holding back. Were the summers dry, the winters abnormally harsh? Whatever the cause, these tightly bunched rings reveal adversity.

But then, still farther out, the rings resume their prosperous spacing, mute memories of better days. Here, indelibly, are written the memoirs of triumph and outreach, the journals of rampancy and joy.

The lesson of the logs is clear.

Life endures. Troubles come, but troubles also go. And life goes on.

The Message in the Dust

We were out there early in the morning, my boy and I, to hunt the wily grouse. The sun was still snoozing below the line of tamarack trees to the east and the predawn air swirled with frigid mists and vapors.

We walked in silence, our footfalls dampened by the dew. From somewhere far away came the ancient warnings of crows. A clique of chickadees passed overhead, the flurry of their wings audible in the stillness, and settled en masse into a young red pine. A blue jay cried indignantly from a birch branch.

We walked along, flexing our fingers against the cold. I gestured toward a spider web strung with pearls of dew. A quaking aspen, sensitive to winds that coarser trees don't notice, fluttered its leaves. Three or four shook loose and seesawed earthward, their pale yellow sides ablaze with light from the rising sun.

"Look," said my son. "A pileated woodpecker." I followed his outstretched hand and saw the great bird beating its way westward, heard its jungle-movie cry, watched as it landed on the skeletal branch of a dead pine and began hammering away in search of food.

Time hung suspended in the golden light of dawn. We came out of the woods onto a sand road and followed it toward the sun. Then we came upon the tracks.

Bear tracks. We bent to inspect them closer. The larger prints were easily seven inches long, the smaller three. The smaller tracks flanked the larger on each side. An adult and two cubs. The skidding sunlight cast the tracks in sharp relief. Fresh tracks, unmistakably.

We followed them backward to where they had emerged from the woods, and in the process came upon the tracks of other creatures. Deer, squirrel, rabbit, grouse; field mice and centipedes; the twisting squiggle of a snake.

Later, heading home, a grouse exploded into flight and I swung the gun stiffly, arthritically, too late.

No matter. We had limited out on things other than grouse. We had witnessed the world being recreated at dawn, seen the magic of sunlight on dew. We had seen at first hand the mystery of dying leaves. We had pondered the marvel of tracks in the sand, surely the source of man's inspiration to write characters and letters with charcoal or stylus or quill. We had resumed, for a while, our rightful place as brothers to the other forms of life.

We had deciphered the message in the dust.

Narrative

In the fall of 1988 we began work on a stone building down next to our marsh, and the following fall opened it for business as a bed-and-breakfast. Over the ensuing decade we welcomed a steady procession of guests to The Stonehouse, many of who returned several times and became dear friends. That same fall our son left home to attend forest-harvesting classes at the vo-tech school in Duluth.

The following summer, we hired a local excavator to dig a pond below the hill north of our house and I began clearing a network of walking trails around our thirty acres to serve as a means of getting firewood and allowing guests to hike. We planted the trails with clover in hopes of attracting more grouse. Through the years since we'd moved here, the thick stands of broomstick-sized popple had thinned themselves into a handsome woods, and many of the hundreds of pine and spruce seedlings we'd planted were beginning to look like respectable trees. When in November the Berlin Wall fell and the Cold War neared its end, a deepening serenity seemed to settle upon our little homestead.

Triumphal Return

O f the many beauties and benefits of living here in the north woods, none can top the springtime arrival of migrating birds.

There is something about the ancient pattern that satisfies the deepest hunger of the spirit. And to know that in many cases the creatures landing in your shrubbery have traveled thousands of miles to get here makes their presence even more delightful.

Over the past several weeks, starting in the latter part of March, a variety of species have graced our acreage and gladdened our winter-weary hearts. I list them in order of appearance, with notes from my hastily scribbled journal.

Robin. The classic sign of spring.

Osprey. Returning to the "home place" high atop a power pole, a location they've used for at least fifteen years. But the nest was destroyed in a windstorm last fall. We waited anxiously to see what would happen. After a couple of weeks of seeming indecision, the ospreys began building a new nest, precisely on the site of the old one.

Juncos. On March 22, under skies which threatened rain, an energetic gang of little grey birds swooped down onto our front lawn and began picking away at sunflower seeds fallen from the winter bird feeder.

Two nights later our family rushed outside at the sound of geese overhead. When we looked up we could see no geese, but were treated instead to a nifty display of northern lights!

The next day, down by the marsh, my wife saw a red-winged blackbird.

On April 3, just at dusk, I chanced upon a phoebe inspecting the eaves of a shed for a possible nesting site. Elegant, shy, and excellent builders, phoebes strike me as having real class.

On Saturday, April 6, while marveling at the 70-degree temperature, I saw a pair of bluebirds looking over one of the bluebird houses we put up a few years ago. How do they know it's for them?

Over the ensuing weeks, the incoming bird traffic increased to near frenzy. Ducks, geese, herons, bitterns, coots, hawks, eagles, crows, and even a pair of pheasants appeared. The abnormally warm temperatures no doubt contributed to the airborne congestion, as the first insects and buds began to emerge. On a single day, the 9th of April, we welcomed chipping sparrows, fox sparrows, flickers, evening grosbeaks, Canada geese, two woodcock, and a mourning dove.

Throughout the balance of April the weather alternated between spring-like hopefulness and throwbacks to winter. But the birds kept on coming. On April 20 I saw a black-and-white warbler perched high in an old popple tree. A few days later turkey vultures floated overhead. On the 27th frogs began peeping down in the marsh.

And then, on the 2nd of May, we were thrilled to hear the evening crooning of a whippoorwill.

Cynics say the two sure things are death and taxes. Fortunately, there are other, lighter, pleasanter things. Things with beaks and feathers and tonic for the soul. Each year they return, completing the ageless circle, unaware of taxes, intent on building nests and bringing to life a whole new brood of babies, thus to triumph over death.

Scratching the Surface

Life in the country, as all rural folks know, involves a lot of work.

Some of the tasks aren't particularly fun. Cleaning out the barn hardly ranks as recreation. Staggering along behind a lawn mower on a 90-degree day falls short of ecstasy. Pulling garden weeds has never really made me hum. These are the kind of jobs you try to Tom Sawyer-off onto the kids; one selling point being that they build character.

Other jobs, however, make a person glad to be alive. For me, grading the driveway is flat out joy.

To blade your road correctly, conditions must be right. Dust does not retain its shape, but damp earth does. So you wait till right after it rains, then get to work.

Supper is long past. I slurp a final cup of coffee and walk to the shed. The '50s vintage Ferguson starts on the first try. I put it into gear, lower the blade, and start down the half-mile of rutted roadway. A few adjustments to get the tilt right, a stop or two to check results, then on up the hill toward the lowering sun and an evening of gentle satisfaction.

Putting along in second gear gives you plenty of time to inspect the world. Here a clump of columbine, there some black-eyed Susans, over there a spray of wild roses, pink against a sea of green.

A young buck deer stares at the tractor and, as I pass, I stare right back. He stands resplendent in the rich light of the setting sun, his newly grown antlers sprouting up like tiny moss-covered trees upon his head. He watches till I'm nearly to the end of the neighbor's field, then lowers his head and resumes his grazing.

Further along I pass a clump of chokecherry trees thick with masses of green cherries. Later, when the summer heat turns the cherries purple-black, the trees will be mauled by the bear who roams these parts, but for now they are fit and vigorous.

On the return trip the woods are noticeably darker, trees and brush blending together into a shadowy mass. At the edge of the field the young buck looks up, freezes, then whirls and bounds away, his white tail pluming up and down like froth on the surface of unseen waves.

Half an hour later, midway through the second pass, a little swarm of insects forms above the hood of the tractor and moves forward through the air in precise synchronization with the machine. Flitting and swooping in foot-wide circles, the bugs swirl through the twilight like specks of dust caught in a tiny tornado.

Looking back, I'm startled to see sparks shooting out from beneath the blade, ignited by the friction of steel against rock. They've been there all along, I realize; only now in the gathering darkness they are visible.

101

I turn once again at the end of the road and start on the final trip toward home. Mists have formed above the hayfields. The tractor motor mutters along, hypnotizing, peaceful. A half-grown cottontail waits as I approach, then explodes in a zigzag frenzy of evasion. The steady hiss of the gravel beneath the blade lulls away all cares.

It's past ten when I pull the old tractor into its shed and climb back down to the ground. Two hours have passed; two hours of my life have been spent scratching the surface of many things, including the back of old Mother Earth. After the next big rain I'll have to redo all that I've just done.

And that's fine by me.

The Pond

One month ago we had a little pond dug in the hollow down below our barn. We'd been dreaming and planning and talking about having it done for years. Then Saturday came and the excavator pulled in with his giant power hoe and late that afternoon the pond was dug.

Our pond will win no prizes for vastness of breadth or profundity of depth. It's basically shaped like a doughnut, with an island where the doughnut hole would be, and averages three to four feet deep. When the digging was finished, the bottom of the excavation was little more than moist. What we had was a hole in the ground encircled by a mound of peat and dirt and broken alder branches. But it was already, in our eyes, a thing of great beauty—and we were confident water would seep in eventually.

Sunday we dragged an old bench down to the edge of our new indentation and spent part of the afternoon watching the water begin to ooze over the bottom. (Where else but in the country could you experience such recreation?) While we watched, birds busied themselves searching for treats in the newly piled dirt and a frog or two ventured into the fledgling lakelet. At dusk two woodcocks gyrated down from the sky and landed quite calmly right next to our feet.

Each evening for the next two weeks we walked down the hill to our pond. "What do you think?" we would ask one another. "I think the level's up another inch," we would say. As the water rose, the little pond grew more and more attractive. We sat on our bench and gazed at the young tamaracks growing on the island, marveling at their perfect reflections in the peat-stained water and feeling the day's tensions ease away into the newly formed reservoir of joy.

One day my brother, Dick, saw a great blue heron wading in the water. Another day we bought a little wooden boat and launched it into the pond, where it rode high and light, as graceful as a floating leaf.

We began to plan new rounds of projects, all springing from the pond. A curving bridge to arch across the water to the island. A three-sided shelter with a fire pit in front, for picnics in the summer and skating in the winter. A little dock for the boat. An old log protruding from the shore to make a place for turtles to enjoy the sun. And somewhere a place for the weeping willow tree my wife has waited for so patiently these many years.

All this will take time. Some of the projects may never reach fruition. But there is no sense of urgency, not down there next to the still waters of our month-old pond.

There everything proceeds at a seeping pace, gentle and calm and quite serene. Once in a while the wind ripples the surface and sends the yellow aspen leaves on miniature excursions toward the island, or prompts a fine drizzle of golden tamarack needles to sprinkle down onto your hair. But even these tempests are tranquil, for we've discovered that the bowl we had carved into the earth has filled not only with water, but also with peace.

Our Better Half

Plants, as every school kid knows, are utterly vital to human life. Without plants we would neither eat nor breathe.

On the undersurface of every leaf a million movable lips are steadily engaged in devouring carbon dioxide and expelling oxygen, thus making it possible for members of the animal kingdom to carry on life.

Of the 450 billion tons of food we humans consume each year, the bulk comes from plants, which synthesize it out of air and soil with the help of sunlight. The remainder of our food comes from animal products, which, in turn, are derived from plants.

From crib to coffin, man relies on cellulose as the basis for his shelter, clothing, fuel, fibers, furniture, cordage, and the paper on which he prints his Bibles and textbooks and magazines. When you add to this list the thousands of items now derived from petroleum (which itself derives from plants), it is clear that our dependency on green things is pushing 100 percent.

But plants do more than satisfy our material needs. Most of us are happiest when living close to them. At birth, marriage, and death, blossoms abound. We give plants and flowers as tokens of love, and use them to grace our altars. Our houses are adorned with gardens, our cities with parks, our nations with forest preserves. Our notion of paradise is that of a garden or bower, luxuriant, sweet-smelling, serene.

Given all of this, it seems surprising that most of us know very little about our green benefactors. We trample on them, chop them down, whack them with weed-eaters, spray them with poisons, and treat them as if they had no feelings.

But they do.

Experiments over the last three decades have established beyond doubt that plants are capable of distinguishing sounds inaudible to the human ear and color wavelengths (such as infrared and ultraviolet) invisible to the human eye. The Indian licorice, for example, is so keenly sensitive to all forms of electrical and magnetic influences that it is used as a weather plant, capable of predicting cyclones, hurricanes, tornadoes, earthquakes, and volcanic eruptions.

Some researchers now suspect that plants have a way of communicating with the outer world that is superior to our five senses. As every gardener knows, plants are quite aware of what they like and don't like, and flourish when their needs are met. And they are capable, to large extent, of regenerating damaged parts, which indicates the presence of some sort of intelligence that directs their actions.

In sum, evidence now supports the vision of the poets, who from ancient times have seen plants as living, breathing, communicating creatures, endowed with personality and certain attributes of soul.

Plants deserve our deepest gratitude and respect. From our viewpoint as members of the animal kingdom, one might say they are our better half. They sustain us in ways we are only beginning to comprehend and ride the earth with us in gentle companionship, giving much more than they take.

Old Photos

As part of the continuing commitment our family has to rid the premises of clutter, we recently decided to organize our old photos.

We have been talking about doing this for several years. But each time we work up the necessary enthusiasm, reality intrudes and causes us to give up.

Thing is, we've got a lot of photographs. Twenty-four years worth, since the "I do's" were spoken. Photographs of family, photographs of friends, photographs of trips, of pets, of flowers, of sunsets, of autumn trees, of snowdrifts, of various vehicles, of grouse hunts, of lunker fish, etc.

Fortunately, we managed to write the date and subject matter on the back of several dozen of these shots.

Unfortunately, we neglected to do so on the remaining several thousand.

Back in the early days of our marriage, we were quite well organized. Besides, we could only afford a roll or two of film per year. But little by little life became more complicated, and we began to take more pictures. Somewhere down the line, we fell behind in our organizational efforts and began to toss whole packets of photos into a large dresser drawer.

Later we needed the dresser for something else and transferred the photos to several large cardboard cartons, which is where they've been resting for the past several years, harmless, uncataloged, inert.

And so they might have remained forever, had Memorial Day not been rainy and cold.

Our daughter, Kia, made the suggestion. "Why don't we get the photos organized?"

"Why not?" said my wife. "After all, it's Memorial Day. Besides, the weather's yucky."

Thus began a task that, should it ever be brought to completion, will probably entail more hours of labor than the building of the pyramids or maybe even the Great Wall of China.

Our plan sounded delightfully simple. First we would zip through the cartons of photos and get them organized by year, eliminating the obvious trash as we went. Then, later, we would shuffle each year's worth into sequential order, scribble notes on the backs, and mount them in good-quality albums. Clearly it would take some time, but what the heck. We'd be creating a photographic memorial to the life and times of the Nagel clan. Surely such a worthy goal deserved a bit of effort.

So we commenced. At first we *ooohhed* and *aaahhed* at the snapshots of the kids when they were little. Then we began having trouble agreeing on what was taken when. Coffee breaks became more frequent. Kia left to go babysitting. The dining room table disappeared under a mishmash of photos and negatives and notes.

Somewhere down the line we began running into bags full of old family photos, given to us as keepsakes by parents and relatives on both sides.

"So now what?" asked my wife. "Some of these go back before the turn of the century. We don't have 24 years of photos here. We've got about a hundred."

Visions of flames danced in my head. "We could burn them," I said. "And while we're at it, we could burn the newer ones too. Or maybe we could bale them all together and saturate them with gasoline and go firebomb the corporate offices of Kodak."

"Get real," said my wife.

So we did.

Now all the "recent" shots are snug inside 24 big envelopes, sorted roughly by years, and the old family heirlooms are resting in their own special carton, to await some rainy day and the reawakened zeal of our daughter.

Memorial Day moved into the past, and after my wife and I started speaking to one another again, we both agreed that one good thing could be said about the holiday. For the first time in years, we had taken no photographs.

Wild Things

The other night while we were eating supper a deer came walking up to our garage.

Naturally, we were surprised. Eating was forgotten while we leaned toward the window, straining to see our unexpected visitor before it decided to leave. Even after it had disappeared back into the woods, we found ourselves spellbound, caught up in the web of mystery and uncertainty that wild creatures create in their wake.

For they do seem, in a way, to be creatures in a dream. They manage to materialize, as if suddenly assembled out of dust motes and beams of light; and just as strangely do they go.

I remember once, some years ago, walking through the woods with my son just after dawn. It was in the early fall and the dew was heavy and quieted our steps upon the path. We were seeking the elusive grouse. Instead, as if by magic, a coyote appeared in the path before us.

We stood still as stumps, almost forgetting to breathe, awestruck by the presence of the tawny apparition there before us. It, too, stopped for just an instant, turning to view us, caught in a shaft of sunlight. Beads of dew sparkled on its fur, creating a corona of spangled light. For a moment its eyes seemed to glow yellow-gold. And then without a sound it was gone.

Had I been alone, I might have thought I was hallucinating, so quickly had it come and gone. But my son had seen it too, and together we managed to reassure ourselves that what we had seen was real, and not some phantom vision or mirage.

Wild things have a unique capacity to surprise us, to startle us out of our ordinary reveries and make us really see. Most of the time we walk about not really looking at our surroundings. The sidewalk is there beneath our feet; we needn't fear stepping into quicksand or onto the back of a sleeping crocodile. The signal light tells us when it's safe to cross the street; the alarm clock tells us when to wake; the thermostat turns on the furnace if the wind shifts to the north.

We move through life seeing only what we choose to see, and most of what we see is man-created.

But wild things snap us out of our dullness and jerk our eyes back to the ancient and abiding realities. They claw holes in the curtains of our smug illusions. They agitate our blood and raise our hackles, and they soothe us and make us calm in ways that man-made things cannot.

We need wild things. We will always benefit from having other creatures, undomesticated, ready in an instant to startle us and make us truly see. They are, as less "civilized" people have always known, our brothers and sisters. Without them life can never be complete.

Walls

Knocking some holes in a wall is rarely an event that rivets the attention of the world.

When the wall happens to be located in Berlin, however, the act of demolition generates great interest.

For nearly three decades we have lived with the numbing presence of the Berlin Wall. It has stood, in reality and in symbol, as one of the world's starkest emblems of fear and hate. Now, abruptly, the terrible partition has been breached.

From both sides of the wall the reaction has been loud and festive. East Berliners have poured by the hundreds of thousands into the west, to see, to greet, and to shop. And their counterparts in West Berlin have strolled, skeptical and astonished, into that part of town that for all these years has been regarded as a province of the Evil Empire.

There is no doubt about the tonic effect this interchange is having on the world. In place of terror there is curiosity. Gunfire is supplanted by good wishes. Distrust is dissolving, giving way to dialogue.

All of which makes me wonder if we haven't a splendid object lesson unfolding before our eyes.

We all spend some of our energy putting up walls. Unlike the Berlin Wall, our walls tend to be invisible. But they are walls, nonetheless, erected to keep others at bay. Some we build quite consciously; these are walls of active hate. Others we simply borrow. These include existing barriers such as racial and religious bias, and the many social judgments regarding class, sex, age, etc. Still others, usually personal, we allow to spring up like a hedge: instead of replying to a letter, we let it go unanswered; instead of reaching out, we draw in.

Whatever the types of walls, one thing is certain—they hurt and restrict us at least as much as they do the party on the other side. These walls cut us off from large parts of life. They box us in. They stifle circulation. In time, they confine and smother us.

If the breaching of the Berlin Wall is to have personal meaning for us, we might use it as an opportunity to begin knocking holes in our self-made partitions. The more holes we make, the more whole our lives become. Instead of hiding, we can reach out, open up, grow. By tearing down the barriers that segregate and separate us from other human beings, we let in great drafts of fresh air for everyone.

I consider it no accident that the words holey, wholly, and holy sound the same. All three words connote health and prompt a sense of celebration.

We are, after all, one species: human.

And we share one home: the planet earth.

Not That Bad

We went cross-country skiing, my wife and I, eager to inspect our corner of the world and get some exercise in the process. The air was warm, the wind was still, and even though we hadn't skied for some time, we were soon making satisfactory progress.

We huffed our way up the big hill south of our house, then left the driveway and started overland along the power-line cut. Within a few minutes we came upon a multitude of fresh deer tracks, stitched into the snow as if by a giant sewing machine. The meandering patterns seemed more playful than purposeful, like the footprints of school kids at recess.

Farther on we came to a patch of brown dirt that proved to be the top of a gopher mound shaved clean by the abrasion of a snowmobile track. The dark hump stood out starkly against the surrounding field of white, a little bonanza of minerals and grit for rabbits and grouse, its surface thawed by sunshine.

We continued on for a quarter-mile or so, then swung to the left down a road through the woods. Here, under cover of young red and jack pine, rabbit tracks ran everywhere. Nibbled brush and scattered scat proclaimed this to be bunny heaven. A grouse exploded from the snow just off the edge of the road and whirred upward to a distant branch. Recent excavations gave evidence of squirrels at work, their presence underscored by a network of tracks connecting the scattered oak trees.

Later we saw the weatherworn hulk of a long-dead popple and stopped to examine the pile of finger-length wood chips at its base, chiseled from the trunk by a pileated woodpecker. Gazing upward at the rhythmic arrangement of holes and furrows cut into the wood, I couldn't help but wonder if such a sight might have inspired a few of our prehistoric ancestors to try their hands at sculpture.

We came at length to where the road joined our driveway, and swung to the east toward home. Near the top of the first hill we stopped to rest, and saw to our delight that the snowbanks on both sides of the road were peppered with snow fleas. We stared at the fidgety black acrobats for some time, wishing we had thought to bring a magnifying glass along.

Finally we pushed on, slowing now and then to marvel at a delicate lacing of mouse tracks, the hip-hop patterns left by the feet of foraging songbirds, the occasional imprint of blue jay wings. Crows called back and forth in the distance, discussing something we couldn't understand. Then we were gliding down the hill we had climbed at the beginning, and a few minutes later we loosened the bindings and stepped out of our skis.

Inside, leaning up against the warm stones of the fireplace, hands wrapped around a steaming cup of coffee, it occurred to me that living in the boondocks isn't really all that bad. Not even in the winter.

Narrative

The '90s brought more change. Kia graduated from high school and went off to college at the University of Minnesota-Duluth. Chris got a job with an area sawmiller, purchased land, and began building a house. A year later he moved into his house and the year after that arranged to buy the sawmill from his employer. Kia graduated from college and began teaching art at St. Peter High School. Our nest was decidedly empty. To compensate, we began inviting more friends and relatives to visit. As time and money permitted, we took to going on longer trips, both here in the states and also abroad. Each year brought an ever-larger number of graduations, weddings, births, and funerals. In '95 Christopher married Sara Barnett. In '96 Kia said "I do" to Rick Holbeck, and my parents celebrated their 60th anniversary. Later that year, Claire and I drove east to Pennsylvania to visit a long-lost cousin and take an extended tour of Frank Lloyd Wright's masterpiece, Fallingwater. I'd been intrigued with Wright's work for decades and tried to incorporate his insights into my own buildings. Over the years we'd visited dozens of his works, and each time we found something new to think about. Fallingwater was no exception.

Doors Into Time

"The odds," said James Thurber, "are on objects." Not people, not ideas, not feelings, but objects. The glory of ancient Egypt fades into oblivion, and with it the fame of its mighty pharaohs. The Sphinx and the pyramids remain.

A bleak thought, perhaps. But taken on the short term, and applied to one's immediate surroundings, Thurber's observation brings unexpected joy. At the domestic level objects have a way of linking you with times gone by.

On the way to the barn to check for eggs I see an elderly aspen tree and notice signs of decay. When I step closer I see a rusted nail protruding from the trunk and immediately my mind snaps back to yesteryear.

That nail, I recollect, once held a skull on its then-shiny shank. The skull of a northern pike, proudly mounted for display by our son, the fisherman. As I recall, Christopher was six or seven when he nailed up the fish head for all to see. Now he's a grown man and a sawmiller who has unkind things to say about people who put nails in trees.

I turn away, smiling at the memories of those early fishing exploits, and move on toward the barn, only to see the weatherworn form of the old Minnesota No. 3, a horse-drawn mower we bought years ago from an elderly gent east of Backus. Looking at the faded red paint, I see in my mind's eye the old man grinning as he explains how the mower works. I hear the musical lilt of his Swedish-American voice, listen to him describe the ratchety clatter of the gears and the jingle of the horses' harnesses and the whisper of the hay as it falls to the advancing sickle bar. This object conjures up a memory within a memory—my memory of the old man and his memory of cutting hay behind the horses.

I fetch the eggs, return to the house, and sit down at the dining-room table. Again, the object works its magic. This table was built from wide pine planks given us by an uncle many years ago. It was designed and put together by my father-in-law, with assistance from my wife and me. On its surface, faintly visible in spite of two resandings, are the dimpled marks of the meat tenderizer our daughter Kia once used to practice drumming, somewhere around age three. Now she's married to a musician and has learned to differentiate between meat tenderizers and drumsticks, but the scars in the wood will always bring forth recollections of her childhood enthusiasm.

And so it goes. Everywhere you look your eye sees objects, and dwelling within each one are memories galore. The nail in the tree, the old mower, the dented table serve as doors into time, allowing you access to the memories of people and events which might otherwise be forgotten.

The odds are on objects.

So be it.

Bonny

Three weeks ago a newcomer joined our family.

Her name is Bonny, she's an English springer spaniel, and her presence has altered our lives. Aside from the expected excitement of pre-dawn risings and watching where you put your foot before you step, she's brought into our home a fascinating study in the art of living.

It is said that the ancient Chinese sage Lao-tzu once decided to observe the behavior of young animals in the hope of finding the secrets of naturalness and joy. Young ones, he felt, exhibited uncommon happiness and seemed always at ease, traits which he wished to accentuate in his own life.

What he found was precisely what Bonny has been trying to teach us: *play* is the thing.

From the six a.m. nip at the tassels of your slippers to the just-before-midnight tug at the hem of your robe, Bonny (like all young creatures) plays.

Put the food in her dish and presto! it's time to dive in and get Puppy Chow smushed into all facial crannies. A drink of water transforms her pendant brown ears into dishrags. A side order of Kibbles and Bits becomes a game on the order of marbles, with nuggets of food rolling all over the floor.

Take her outside and the game intensifies. She plays tag with a skittering leaf, holds a captive twig upright between oversize paws, rolls a newfound stone back and forth with her nose. Then abruptly, as if responding to some whispered cosmic alert, she abandons the stone and commences to race in frenzied circles around the yard, running as fast as her gangly legs will carry her, ears flapping like the wings of a bird, a bright shining madness in her eyes, as if she were trying to show us the path toward enlightenment. ("It's this way, you dullards. It's round and round as fast as can be and full of good cheer and much panting.")

But there is more here than just play.

There is curiosity. Curiosity without bounds. Bonny is interested in **everything**.

From the first spring moth to a cocoon nestled in the siding of the house to a discarded sunflower seed beneath the bird feeder, she is eager to examine, eager to sniff and taste and learn.

And there is flexibility, suppleness, hanging loose. Running pell-mell across the yard with a stolen plastic bag clamped in her teeth, she managed the other day to land her front paws on the bag, which instantly jerked her head earthward. The result? A perfect somersault. By going with the moment, rather than resisting it, she turned a potential disaster into yet another celebration.

When Bonny is tired, she sleeps.

When she's hungry, she eats.

Whatever she's doing, she does it with gusto, with abandon.

In the short time she's been with us, she's moved steadily into our hearts and just as steadily into our minds. Could it be that she was sent to teach us how to live? Is it her destiny to play the role of resident guru?

If so, we're open to becoming her disciples.

Lord knows, we have much to learn.

Saturday Morning

Saturday morning, 8 a.m., March 12.

I sit in the screened porch with a cup of coffee and listen to the sounds of an awakening world.

Is it my hope, projected onto the ice-locked landscape, or is it a fact that things seem warmer today, less brittle, easing toward spring?

I sip from the steaming cup and listen to the wind washing through the pine boughs. Today the sound is softer, more pliant, filled with a sensuous sighing. Perhaps the pine needles, released from the rigid grip of frost, are more receptive to the movement of the wind.

A chickadee swoops toward the feeder, wing beats audible in the magic air. A huff, a glide, again a little huff, and it sails to a perfect landing on the edge of the seed-filled tray. Breakfast al fresco, unhurried, serene. No schedule looms to shadow the joy of breaking fast. I wish for an instant I too could sweep through the air, seed in beak, to perch upon a popple branch and savor a morning tidbit.

In the distance I hear a clamoring of crows. Crows! Those black-cloaked bringers of spring, officious and blustering like bureaucrats come to oversee some dedication. They move nearer, boisterous but unseen, and again my pulse speeds at the thought of winter being overthrown.

Coffee gone, I step into the house for a refill, and see atop the old wood cookstove a vase my wife has filled with forsythia branches. A good friend left these branches, bundled, on top of our mailbox last week, along with a note wishing us well. Now the buds are beginning to swell, little flames of vivid yellow, and in a day or two they will burst open into a spray of delicate petals. I touch the rough skin of the twigs and tickle the tip of a bud and marvel at the miracle before me.

There are times when the world feels badly out of joint. The follies of human misbehavior fill the TV screen and blare from the radio every hour. Our hearts ache at the inequities and injustices paraded before us. Our minds darken with fears of a worsening future.

In the meantime, with little fanfare, winter drips away into spring and the earth prepares itself to green again. Chickadees begin to look for mates, buds prepare to open, and the ancient cycle of birth-life-death-and-rebirth wheels its magnificent way through the eons.

A Mystery Explained

Ever wonder why on some days things go less well than on others?

We've all had them—those days when, unaccountably, we stumble over our own feet, days when our strength deserts us, days when molehills swell into mountains, days when we drop things.

There are many theories purporting to explain such days, but only one that explains them well.

Forget what you've read about biorhythms. Discard the superstitions about gremlins. Discount such factors as humidity, barometric pressure, or phases of the moon.

What we're talking about, folks, is gravity. That mysterious tug all objects possess; the affinity of apples for earth made famous by Sir Isaac Newton.

According to Newton's law of gravitation, any two particles of matter in the universe attract each other with a force varying directly as the product of their masses and inversely as the square of the distance between them. The larger the mass, the stronger the pull; the greater the distance between objects, the less the pull.

It's hard to imagine what life must have been like before Newton came along and enlightened the world to the extent that he did. Folks everywhere must have been wary of apples, expecting them now and then to fly upward or sideways rather than fall down. Once Sir Isaac got things sorted out, people could relax a little and avoid the undersides of fruit trees.

But mysteries remained. From the time of Newton's major publication in 1687, nearly three more centuries passed before the novelist Kurt Vonnegut, Jr., published his findings about gravitational force. Newton, said he, had failed to notice one tremendously important point: the gravitational force varies from day to day.

Now, thanks to Vonnegut, we are able to make sense of a whole raft of vexations that puzzled our forebears. Once we understand that the force of gravity fluctuates, all kinds of things begin to fall into place.

Remember when you last stubbed your toe or bit the edge of your tongue? That, friends, happened on a Heavy Gravity Day. Or when you dropped your cup of coffee in your lap, or failed to toss the crumpled Kleenex all the way to the wastebasket? Another HGD.

Men: do you see now why, on occasion, your belly hangs over your belt? Why the shot you took at that duck last fall was so low? Why you couldn't beat out that infield hit in the softball game?

Ladies: do you understand, finally, why some days it seems your foundation-wear provides insufficient support? Why the cake failed to rise? Why last Tuesday the vacuum cleaner seemed made of cement?

Heavy Gravity Days. Days when the flowers droop and the car gets poor mileage and everything seems so damned difficult.

And, conversely, Light Gravity Days, when there's a spring in your step and a buoyancy in your heart, when things leap to hand and the grass grows two inches overnight.

Isn't it wonderful knowing?

Reflections

All things considered, robins are wonderful birds.

They're common as gravel and humbly appointed, disdaining the flash of the oriole or the aerial tricks of the hummingbird.

They sing quite beautifully but spend most of their time at work, extracting worms from the earth and winging them up to their ravenous young.

They get down to business early each spring and stick around our parts till late fall, and when they depart they do so quietly, a few at a time, foregoing the theatrics of massed migration.

Robins are solid, dependable, middle-class. But every so often one of them goes awry. A few years back we were harassed by such a robin. It started down by the garage with a strange *tink tink tink*.

"What's that?" asked my wife.

"A *tink*, I think."

"Obviously," she said. "But what's making it?"

Investigation revealed a robin bent on attacking a hubcap. When I reported my findings, my wife seemed skeptical. "But why?"

I returned to the driveway and resumed my detective work, concealed behind an oak tree several feet from the parked car. The robin, I noted, seemed fixated on the right front wheel. It hopped around in a circle, came back to the wheel, jumped into the air, and stabbed the hubcap with its beak. It took several *tinks* before the light went on. The robin was attacking its own reflection.

Given this news, my wife nodded. "Makes sense," she said. "He must think it's an intruder. Robins are very territorial."

A year later, in spring, we were awakened by a *tink* against glass. For a moment I thought my mind had drifted back to childhood when, like Huck Finn and the boys, we'd wake a sleeping comrade by tossing a pebble against his bedroom window. Then the *tink* came again. When I opened the curtain I saw it was a robin.

Hubcaps are one thing. If the *tink* gets too irritating, you can pull the car into the garage and shut the door. But getting roused from sleep morning after morning after morning at an unseemly hour is another. We tried various remedies and finally settled on a blanket tacked over the outside window frame.

The year after that the robin, or one of its descendants, came again. This time thoughts of homicide bubbled in my brain. I dusted off my trusty 12-gauge and jacked a shell into the chamber.

"You can't shoot a songbird," said my wife.

"I can if I lead it enough."

As it turned out the robin went away, perhaps aware in some extrasensory way of my dark intentions.

In the years since I have pondered the seeming insanity of attacking one's own reflection and come to realize how often we humans indulge in similar behavior. For us it takes more complicated forms, but the principle's the same.

We start by projecting our flaws onto someone else—a spouse, a child, a co-worker, a politician, a neighbor. Then we commence to find fault. "He's so insensitive." "She's such a slob." "Why can't you pay more attention to me?" "What a klutz!" Seething with righteous anger, we level our lances and gallop into battle, eager to rid the world of evil.

Like the robin doing battle with a hubcap, we fail to see things clearly, and never guess that what we're fighting are reflections of our own imperfect selves.

Beware the Ice Cream Pail

For many months a motley pile of notes, receipts, photos, letters, and assorted bric-a-brac lay piled upon my desk.

Whenever the spirit moved or inclement weather allowed, I'd chip away at the pile, answering a letter, filing a batch of receipts, scribbling notes on the backs of photos before putting them away. The system would have made a lazy man proud and given an efficiency expert chest pains.

I say, "would have," because, in a frenzy of spring-cleaning madness, I decided to clean up the mess. I tossed a lot of things in the wastebasket, put a few where they belonged, pitched the rest into an ice cream pail (the handiest container I could find), and shoved the pail into a corner near the wall.

Tidiness triumphed: for the first time in recent memory, my desk was clean.

But as the next several days passed I began to notice something disturbing: I was no longer chipping away. My desire to respond to the letters in the ice cream pail had vanished, as had the impulse to reread notes, file receipts, and scribble on the backs of photos.

By putting everything into one handy receptacle, I had somehow lost all sense of connection with the contents.

Several days later I saw a program on TV about the hundreds of thousands of people starving in Ethiopia. Starving to death, while folks in industrial countries pay money to join weight-loss clinics.

And suddenly I made the connection between the little melodrama on my desktop and the terrifying tragedy in Africa.

Putting things into categories is a natural and efficient thing to do. But when you put them there, you automatically cease to think of them (whether letters or malnourished children) as being real. All sense of encounter is lost, and with it any feeling of importance or urgency.

The human brain is an extraordinary organ. When we use it to focus on individual, specific things, it provides us with incredible sensitivity. But when we use it as a mere computer, a lumper-together-or-sorter-of-data, it paradoxically allows us to become detached and unemotional.

Life is a great and noble mystery comprised of countless little miracles.

The enemy of life is numbness, unreality; a bunch of notes and letters dumped into an ice cream pail and then forgotten.

Summer Nights

O f the many joys that summer brings, some of the best occur at night.

There is something immensely satisfying about sitting on the deck or in the screen porch talking with friends as the sky turns toward purple and the whippoorwill begins to call. Later, when darkness rules, the dots of light appear: stars overhead, fireflies to the side, a candle flame atop the table.

It is then that the conversation grows best and the words, coming from faces barely visible, take on a depth and power otherwise missing.

Not that all talk is about things of surpassing importance. Some of what's said is humdrum. We're getting low on milk again. Don't forget to mail that letter in the morning. Did anyone hear the weather forecast? Any chance of rain?

But on occasion the mood turns serious, and words are measured and weighed before being spoken. What's the best way to oppose terrorism? Where will the terrorists strike next? Why is the world so filled with violence?

Then someone tells a joke or remembers a funny anecdote about Aunt Mabel and laughter wells up out of the darkness and washes away some of our worries.

Another glass of wine? Anybody need another beer? Ice tea? Lemonade? Don't be bashful, folks. It's summertime, remember? Enjoy.

And so the evening passes, voices lapping softly like waves against the shore, rising and falling like the point of flame above the candle on the table, giving you the sense of being passengers aboard an unseen ship moving gently through the night.

Gradually the intervals between words grow longer. Someone yawns. An owl hoots from the woods. A plane drones past above, its warning lights blinking like a high-altitude firefly beckoning to its less daring cousins.

A match is struck and for an instant faces emerge from the darkness. Another person yawns. A joke is told and laughter follows, but the sound of it is softer than before. The candle flame gutters low for a time, flares brightly, then goes out.

"Well, I guess it's about that time."

"Yeah."

"Anybody want to go for a short walk? The stars are really beautiful tonight."

No one replies.

"Oh, well. Probably time to hit the rack anyway."

A chair scrapes. Then another.

"Careful. The dog's lying right in front of you."

"Oh, wow! I would've stepped right on her."

The whippoorwill offers a final chorus and then it is silent again.

"God," someone murmurs. "Summer nights."

Lots of Life

Midsummer. The vital urge nears its zenith. Life is everywhere apparent, everywhere growing and pushing and stretching itself, as if to see how far and how high it can reach.

Each walk down our sand road reveals an embroidery of tracks. Deer tracks, fox tracks, cat tracks, snake tracks, mouse and squirrel and bird tracks—dozens of creatures have been here and gone.

Five minutes spent listening in early morning yields a bouquet of birdsong, ranging from the domestic chitchat of wrens to the plaintive wail of loons to the raucous holler of ill-mannered crows. And speckled here and there among the other sounds are insect hums and the clicks and chitters of chipmunks and squirrels.

In summer life swells to its fullest and glories fill the earth. Each leaf, each flower, each droplet of dew seems full of extraordinary beauty and importance. Even the clouds possess an uncommon complexity and grandeur, as if having finally gained maturity. Slate-hued thunderheads sail majestically past cottony billows of white, while high above diaphanous curtains grace the stratosphere.

A walk in the woods reveals a doe and long-legged fawn, white-spotted and shy. Flies hover about; the ears of the deer flick steadily. Overhead a hawk screes long and loud and soulfully, voicing the fervor of those permitted to soar. A breath of wind and the popple leaves tremble, as if in ecstasy at the invisible lover's touch.

All things are here, now, full. Summer is the summation, the summit, the summons to celebration. Life is full and life is good.

And life is short.

Soon the popple leaves will lose their juiciness and shrivel into husks. Soon the hawk will plummet into the meadow grass and emerge with a young rabbit gripped in its talons. Soon the gawky fawn and her mother will run the hunters' gauntlet and, if they survive, the harsher gauntlet posed by winter.

It is this sense of mortality hovering in the wings that imparts such an aching sweetness to life, that makes your heart swell to the point of explosion. Were life as we see and hear and feel it to last forever, the seasonal rhythms would grow boring, the tracks in the sand diminish to mere squiggles. It is the shortness of it all that lends the sweetness, the vinegar of death that adds the honey to life.

In its summer fullness, life calls out to each of us, cries out in admiration and love. "Behold!" it cries. "Behold the beauty! Fix it fast in your vision, for soon it will be gone!"

Behold!

Cousins

Of the many varieties of formal human relationships, none holds a candle to cousins.

Cousins are the nails that clinch the larger family structure together. They are its haphazard but effective memory bank, its mentor, its conscience, its court jester.

Unique among genealogical—as well as legal—relations, cousins are the down-home, don't-lie-to-me, go-to-the-wall, in-your-face kind of friends that each of us could use a dozen more of (and, if we had them, would probably drive us nuts).

You really can't put much past a cousin. Oh, maybe in the early years, especially if you're the elder. But by the time you hit the acne era, you know whom you can trust and confide in, and who will never let you crawl too far out on the limb of self-delusion. Moms and dads are fine and very necessary, but there are certain things you just can't talk to them about. Cousins, on the other hand, are made for talking to.

You can talk to a cousin about anything, secure in the knowledge that your confidences will not be betrayed. They can't be: not if your cousin remembers what he or she has confided to you. It's a case of mutual—and very functional—blackmail, a miniature model of the "balance of power" that statesmen and historians talk about.

Another splendid quality of cousins is that they never seem to change. You can move away and not see a cousin for 20 years, and then get together and within five minutes you're in the groove again. Oh, sure, once in a while a cousin gets uppity or weird and tries on some ill-fitting form of pretense. But all you need to do is bide your time and discuss the situation with another cousin or two, and the errant one will probably return to the fold.

Cousins are a family's memory. Like the itinerant minstrels of the Middle Ages, they know all the stories, remember all the songs, are acquainted with all the legends. Their shared pool of information is oceanic in size. A cousin can tell you just how it happened that Uncle Fred accidentally squirted Reddi-Wip into that society lady's cleavage at the fund-raising dinner, how Aunt Wendy managed to drive the family car through the back wall of the brick garage, or how Grandpa Will got stuck in the privy seat when he was just a whippersnapper.

As the years roll on, cousins become family advisers, watching out for the welfare of Aunt Minnie at the rest home, nudging the newlyweds toward the right choice of house, sending hand-me-downs to the most recently born. They hover, spirit-like, in the family's background, helping where needed (and sometimes where not).

They are, in sum, the essence of a family. They give a clan its distinctive style, keep it from taking itself too seriously, contribute to its lore. Without cousins, a family just wouldn't be the same; and for each of us, life would be duller by far.

Pilgrimage

We finally did it.

Last week we went to visit Fallingwater, the world-famous house by Frank Lloyd Wright.

Cantilevered over a waterfall in western Pennsylvania, Fallingwater is the stuff of dreams. The American Institute of Architects chose it as the most beautiful residence built in the past 100 years. Some 140,000 visitors come to it annually. Situated in a wooded mountain valley east of Pittsburgh, several miles from the nearest town, this amazing building exerts a magnetism felt round the world.

Fallingwater was constructed in the midst of the Depression, at a time when Wright's career was thought by many to be over. The man was nearing 70 and hadn't had a significant commission in several years. Then a young fellow named Edgar Kaufmann, Jr., showed up at Wright's home in Wisconsin, eager to enroll in the fledgling architectural school Wright and his wife had established a few years earlier. Kaufmann's father, it turned out, owned a flourishing business in Pittsburgh and wanted someone to build him a vacation home on the banks of Bear Run, a cascading stream that ran through several hundred acres of land he owned in the Laurel Valley.

Wright visited the site, asked for a topographical map, and came up with the outrageous—and brilliant—idea of siting the house directly over the top of a waterfall. He called for a set of four piers to be built at the edge of the stream, and atop these piers he cantilevered reinforced concrete decks out over the water. Stacked like a series of trays from one floor to the next, the decks are counterbalanced in place by the tons of native stone used to build the walls and fireplaces, and attached to a rock outcropping behind the house by a row of concrete beams.

The result is pure magic. The house seems to hover in the air above the falls, rising like an apparition to a height of three stories. Bands of glass invite the outside in and turn the inside out. Floors of waxed flagstone echo the stone of the creek bed. A rock outcropping rises up through the floor in front of the living room fireplace, to act as hearth. Inside, the sense of shelter is remarkable. You are embraced by rearward walls of stone while at the same time free to view a panorama of wild trees and shrubs through the floor-to-ceiling glass, an arrangement of such primitive satisfaction as to make you feel invincible. Because of the humidity caused by the cascading water, all interior furnishings are made of black walnut, designed by Wright to echo shapes and angles of the house itself. And everywhere you go, you hear the murmur of the moving water, a sound guaranteed to wash all tension from even the most troubled occupant.

Throughout his long career, Wright insisted that all buildings should draw their inspiration from the natural world, honoring their sites by careful accommodation to existing contours and vegetation, so that they seemed to grow naturally from the earth. He further sought to make his buildings welcome sunshine, orienting them toward the south-southeast and massing their openings into curtain-walls of glass.

"The good building," said Wright, "makes the landscape more beautiful than it was before the building was built."

Fallingwater stands as a testament to the truth of his statement. It is a poem written in stone and glass, celebrating the possibility of man's harmony with nature. This remarkable structure, nestled in an obscure wooded valley above an unnamed waterfall, speaks directly to the deepest longings of the human spirit.

Midnight Walk

I went for a walk at midnight, bundled up against the thirty-below cold. Moonlight cast a webwork of tree shadow on the pale snow. The air hung motionless, as if frozen in place. In the stillness I heard the crack of a tree trunk split by frost, and the distant yipping of a dog. Stars glittered like chips of ice, some of them so far away they might be nonexistent by now, their light still streaming earthward, the glow from a fire long burnt out.

I trudged along, struck by the preposterousness of life. How, in a universe so enormous and so cold, might there be creatures like us, with eyes to look upon the world and nerves to capture sensations and minds to mull over what we see and feel? The odds of such a thing, I thought, are laser thin.

I looked back up at the stars and felt a sudden gratitude. How wonderful, how incredibly sweet, to be alive! For an instant I saw past the labels that confuse us; saw that we are all little packets of life instinctively loyal to our source.

The person picketing against abortions, the environmentalist defending the rights of whales, the doctor struggling to save a gunshot victim, the social worker trying to find funds to feed a hungry family, the farmer putting seeds into the earth, the logger harvesting wood with which to build shelter, the teacher encouraging young minds to blossom, even the health official dispensing condoms in the hope of preventing unplanned pregnancy—all these acts, and thousands of others, spring from a sense of loyalty to life. The way we go about defending life may put us at odds with one another, but the impulse that drives us is the same.

At bedrock, far below the confusing categories that our minds invent and by which we are often blinded, stands the sense of awe, the wordless impulse to give thanks. This ancient sense of the sacredness of life is what gives rise to all religions. At root, the Hindu and the Buddhist and the Muslim and the Christian and the Jew are united; it is only their creeds, their attempts at verbal formulation, that push them apart.

Down deep, all human beings, whether black or white or red or yellow or male or female or young or old or strong or weak or bright or slow, share common ancestry and are, essentially, cousins. But the genealogical records have blurred through time, and now we think we belong to separate races or nationalities or sexes, and mistakenly believe the differences that divide us are greater than the similarities we share. The inability to see that we are all related keeps us from reaching out to one another, and denies us the joy of seeing deep into each other's eyes and celebrating our common humanity.

I stopped walking and listened to the barking dog and felt, again, the sense of relatedness. From the single-celled amoeba to the creepy crawlers, on through the finny forms that swim through water and feathered forms that fly through air, to the four-leggeds that run upon the earth and burrow in its softness and climb upon its body hair (each strand of which we call a tree), to the two-leggeds that strut about thinking they are the crown of creation, all life is one. Life is life is life.

I turned around and started back toward home.

The odds of life existing are awesomely small. The fact that it does is unspeakably grand. To it, and to the improvement of its quality and the protection of its diversity, we owe our deepest loyalty.

Narrative

The first week of 1997 brought nearly two feet of snow, followed by several days of bitter cold. Toward the end of the month the National Guard was mobilized to help dig out the western counties of the state. To help ward off winter's gremlins, I began having long talks with a friend who'd spent the cold months of the last 20 years down in the Bahamas, living aboard his sailboat. Now the boat was in dry dock on the shore of Lake Superior, and up for sale. Tempting, very tempting…but fate had other plans. Spring brought epic floods to the Red River Valley. And summer brought emotional floods to us.

In July, Kia underwent an operation for the removal of an ovarian cyst that turned out to be malignant. Over the next several months our hearts alternately soared and crashed as the cancer advanced, retreated, and advanced again. The day before her golden birthday, November 26, she called to say the cancer had spread, with a tumor in each lung and pinhead-sized spots on her liver, and that she would have to begin chemotherapy in December. But her spirits were upbeat, her joy in life undiminished. Despite the prospect of giving herself daily injections and making frequent trips to the Mayo Clinic, she took profound delight in working with her students and spending weekends visiting friends and going to concerts with her beloved husband, Rick, a talented musician.

At Christmas the whole larger family assembled at our house for an intensive get-together and the chance to spend time with Kia. She presented Claire and me with a beautiful framed print of a black-and-white drawing she'd worked on for weeks. We stayed up late for several nights in a row, talking about times past and her hopes for the future. She and Rick were determined to buy a house in St. Peter and had already begun looking. Somehow she'd beat the cancer and go on to live a long and fruitful life. A week later she called to say the latest X-rays showed that the tumors had shrunk. In early February she announced that the tumors in her lungs had shrunk some more and that the spots on her liver had disappeared, but that a new malignancy was visible in her spine, putting pressure on her spinal cord and causing her right leg to go occasionally numb.

In March she and Rick took the plunge and bought a small but serviceable house, and we drove down to St. Peter to help them move. On St. Patrick's Day Kia underwent surgery to remove the tumor in her spine. Rick called to say the surgeon was able to remove over 90% of the malignancy, and felt hopeful that radiation could eliminate the rest. Kia's fellow teachers volunteered to each give her a day of paid sick leave to cover her recuperation, and the school board agreed to accept their offer. For the first time in weeks, we felt a surge of real hope.

Then, on the last weekend of that month, a tornado roared through the area, destroying their garage and damaging the roof and windows of their newly purchased house. And in early May, X-rays revealed that the tumors in Kia's lungs had grown larger. For nearly a year, we'd all been living on a rollercoaster of rising and falling emotions, hating the presence of the disease and the pain it so ruthlessly inflicted on our dear daughter, praying that somehow it would go away and leave her whole. Now we sensed the wing beats of the Dark Angel, and were barely able to breathe.

On the 19th of June, surrounded by loved ones, she slipped away.

Kia

Our daughter, Kia Naomi, died Friday, June 19, at 9:15 p.m. Kia was 26, a woman in the bloom of life, married not quite two years to her husband, Rick Holbeck. Rick loved her. Kia loved Rick. They both loved life. And now she is gone.

We know how she died. Cancer: a particularly virulent form of ovarian cancer that galloped through her body and settled in her spine and lungs, crowding out the normal cells until there was no way left for her to breathe.

But we don't know why. Why should a young person in rollicking good health suddenly fall prey to such a wasting and painful disease? Why should a gentle, caring woman be forced to endure the ravages of radiation and chemotherapy and surgeries, and in the end die anyway? I don't have answers to these questions, and neither does my wife, and neither did Kia.

What we do know is that she died surrounded by love. There were eight of us around her bed: Claire and I, Rick, his parents, our son, Chris, and his wife, Sara, and Kia's oldest friend, Jenny. We held her hands and smoothed her forehead and urged her to let go, to follow the light, to step across the threshold to the next adventure. The last thing she said to us was, "I love you all very much." A few hours later she was gone.

After her death we set about planning her funeral. We decided that she should be buried in comfortable clothes—her favorite bib overalls, a t-shirt, her sandals—and surrounded by comforting things, including her ever-faithful teddy bear. We considered having a conventional funeral service and chose instead to have a celebration at which her many friends could publicly share their memories. We bought a bunch of brightly colored flags and windsocks to commemorate her cheerfulness. Rick decided he would sing "their song" to her. His brother, Jim, agreed to play guitar. Jenny said she'd read some poetry. And my oldest and dearest friend, Judge Bill Walker, agreed to deliver the eulogy. As a young pastor, Bill had baptized Kia. Twenty-four years later, he had married her to Rick. And now, all too shortly after that, he would preside over her funeral.

On the cover of the program we put a portion of her last art work, which she finished just before she died: two wolves peering out from under a leaning tree trunk. On the inside we chose to print the following, from a letter Dr. Elisabeth Kuebler-Ross once wrote to a child dying of cancer:

When we have passed the tests we were sent to Earth to learn, we are allowed to graduate. We are allowed to shed our body, which imprisons our soul the way a cocoon encloses the future butterfly, and when the time is right we can let go of it. Then we will be free of pain, free of fears and free of worries...free as a beautiful butterfly returning home to God...which is a place where we are never alone, where we continue to grow and to sing and to dance, where we are with those we loved and where we are surrounded with more love than we can ever imagine.

Farewell, sweet princess.

Enjoy your journey.

We love you.

Narrative

In the months following Kia's death, we learned what the phrase "gone but not forgotten" really meant. It meant sleepless, tearful nights during which Claire and I clung to one another like shipwrecked castaways drifting in the sea. It meant whole days of silent and stony depression during which neither of us spoke a word. It meant talking with a counselor as we tried to make sense of something innately senseless. It meant watching TV when a Minneapolis station covered the release of hundreds of butterflies at St. Peter High School in homage to Kia. And it meant an unexpected number of friends and neighbors kind enough to share their memories of our daughter or stories of their own particular heartbreaks. Gradually we learned that we were not alone and that we needed to learn how to let go. This, we decided, would probably take the rest of our lives.

Heads

Sitting in a mall, taking a break from shopping, I suddenly became aware of all the heads.

Usually you see the bodies: big tall skinny guy there, little bent pair of ladies here, nervous bouncy teen girls making cracks about the guys they're pretending not to notice, gloomy middle-aged men being dragged like oversize boys from store to store to store.

But this time I saw the heads, lots of heads, dozens, hundreds, swarms of heads, bobbing and gliding and tilting and rocking, up down up down, turning to stare at the "25% off" signs, stopping, frowning, blinking, thinking, moving on.

Heads. On top of each and every body all around the world there is a head, and inside each head there are a trillion brain cells thinking thoughts, preserving memories, making plans.

No two of these heads are alike.

No two can reveal to one another more than a fraction of what's inside them.

Sitting there, watching all the heads, I realized what a private thing the skull is. Here, perched atop the neck, is a world within the world, round like a planet and as inaccessible as an asteroid. Here, bedecked with hats and hair and sporting an ear on each side, is the ultimate sanctuary, so private and secure it needn't be guarded with fences or gates or No Trespassing signs.

Inside the head the spirit is free to soar and dive and romp and sing. In the utter seclusion of the mind we are at liberty to do and be whatever we wish. Empires are ours for the imagining; daydreams can take whatever form we fancy; witticisms and wisdom abound.

Watching the heads in the mall I wondered: why are these faces (not all, but many) so vapid and glum? Having no mirror, I couldn't see mine, but I knew without seeing that it, too, was dull.

Is it the monotony of malls, the hypnotic shuffle of shopping? I found myself hoping it was.

Seeing a dour-faced lady of uncertain years, I decided she would be different at home. Once in the door she would set her purchases aside and pry off her toe-pinching shoes and go sit down by the fire with a cup of coffee. Then her face would grow warm and relaxed and the ache in her head would subside, and perhaps she would close her eyes and her mind would conjure up memories of times past, good memories filled with laughter and shouts, and she would be glad. And if she could be glad, why couldn't we all?

I got up, feeling much better. "It's all in the head," I thought. "Reality is a state of mind." I looked once more at the galaxy of heads moving about and I knew that what lives within those bone-cradled brains is the horror and the hope of all mankind.

For better or worse, each of us rules the universe that sits atop our shoulders.

No Such Thing as an Average Chickadee

Sitting at lunch one winter day staring at the bird feeder, I was struck by the fact that each bird was distinct from all others.

First, of course, there was the obvious difference from species to species. An evening grosbeak, with its zoot suit of yellow and black, runs no risk of being mistaken for a blue jay or a chickadee. The goldfinches are clearly different from the nuthatches. And even the hairy and downy woodpeckers can be told apart the instant you see them together. The hairy is bigger; much bigger.

But the difference went beyond species lines.

There, scrabbling after the black sunflower seeds, were three chickadees. At first they seemed mere copies of some proto-chickadee, clones from an Ideal Bird. But a closer look made me reconsider.

The one on the left, I saw, was slightly larger than the others, and had a peculiar way of half-turning, half-twisting its head.

The one in the center seemed much more jittery than its companions. Does it suffer from mental upset? Did it fly into the windowpane once too often? Or is it a normal bird, framed by companions much slower than itself?

The more I looked, the more I began to sense the individuality of each of the chickadees. The one on the right, for instance, had a mottled rump, much darker than its feeder mates. And its black beard looked longer than average.

Average? I began to wonder about the word "average." And about the word "normal," too.

Is there really such a thing? How far down its chest does the beard of the "average" chickadee extend? How many times per minute does its heart beat? Which of the three birds was exhibiting "normal" behavior?

Parents who have more than one child know there's no such thing as average or normal, at least not when applied to living people. We can say this child is of average height for his age or that person sleeps an average of nine hours per night, but it's preposterous—and pointless—to say "George is an average fellow," or "Tilly, poor soul, is abnormal."

Nature, which is our mother just as much as the chickadee's, has given each of us peculiarities that set us off from one another. It seems to me that we should be glad of this, and look upon our quirks and eccentricities as sources of delight rather than embarrassment. And I, for one, deplore the efforts made by social scientists to establish norms for any aspect of behavior.

Watching the feeder, the message came clear: there's no such thing as an average chickadee.

Cold Snap

Whoever first coupled the words "cold" and "snap" together knew what he or she was talking about.

There is something about extreme cold that is rigidly connected with snap.

From ten or fifteen degrees below zero on down, everything starts getting that snappy feeling. Your nose, fingers, and toes all hint at snapping off if struck by a sudden blow. The snow beneath your boots snaps and squeaks as if in mortal pain. Things made of plastic (like pails) and things made of thin metal (like car keys) threaten to snap if treated ungently. In the woods at midnight you can hear the trees exploding with frost cracks. And hovering over it all, threatening to splinter into a thousand broken shards, is, of course, your mind.

Whether because of a houseful of cabin-fevered kids or a car battery that has decided to hibernate for the rest of the winter or a water pipe that has gone solid-state, cold snaps bring with them some serious stress. I can remember one winter night back in the early '70s when we lived in the woods many miles from town and our kids were both infants. The mercury in our outdoor thermometer kept creeping downward until it huddled in a ball at the bottom of the bulb marked -45 F. The gas-fired furnace staged a work stoppage and for a while I thought we might have run out of fuel. But when I bundled up and went out to check the LP tank I found it well over half-full.

By midnight the temperature inside the house was in the mid-30s and still going down. We bundled the sleeping kids in cocoons of blankets and decided our only hope was to get the furnace going again. I ran a long extension cord out to the gas tank, plugged in a kerosene heater, and wondered uneasily if the tank might explode. But it didn't, and half an hour later the furnace resumed operation. The next morning we heard from a neighbor that the temperature had bottomed at fifty-something below. Many years later we learned that LP gas stops vaporizing at -44 F, which explained why the fuel wasn't getting to the furnace.

But such isolated memories of cold snaps hardly compare with the rigors others have endured in times past. According to my wife's aunt Alfie, who was born in 1900 and lived all her life on the prairies of North Dakota, the worst winter was 1936, smack in the middle of the Dust Bowl years, or as folks out there call them, the "Dirty Thirties." In that winter, the temperature never climbed above zero for 40 consecutive days, with lows at night of -30 to -40 F.

So no matter how cold it gets here, one can safely assume others living elsewhere have endured much worse. Folks in Siberia, for instance, work all winter in temperatures ranging down to minus 70 F. There it is common to leave taxis and work trucks running continuously from fall till spring, never turning off the motors for fear they might not start again. The key to enduring such cold, they say, is to keep active, keep dry, and think warm.

Personally, I prefer long naps.

Boy and Dog

Call the boy Jeb. Call the dog Sparks. Imagine the boy on the porch, reading a comic. Imagine the dog on the front yard grass, dozing off in the shade of a lilac bush.

A crow caws from a treetop. Jeb looks up, as does the dog. Neither of them can see the crow. But their eyes catch across the expanse of lawn and Jeb murmurs, "Hi, Sparks," and Sparks thumps his tail against the ground.

An utterly common event. But consider what's happened.

One form of consciousness (a boy named Jeb) has communicated through space to a different form of consciousness (a dog named Sparks) and Sparks has communicated back. The forms are separated by, say, 50 feet of distance, and are not connected by wires or pipes or any type of transmitting medium other than air. The vibration of Jeb's vocal cords sent the outgoing message; the movement of Sparks's tail sent the reply.

Jeb's mother calls from the house. "Randy's on the phone. He says he can't wait to talk to you."

Jeb goes inside, grinning. His best friend Randy moved out to the west coast last week, 1,500 miles away. Jeb grabs the receiver and they talk. Two similar forms of consciousness communicate verbally over a distance of several states, connected in this case by lines of copper wire or fiber optics. But midway through the call Randy says his mom needs to make several phone calls. "Just hang up and I'll call you back on the cell phone," he says.

A few minutes later they're talking again, this time connected by nothing but the impulse of radio waves vibrating invisibly through the atmosphere. The boys can't see or touch or feel or smell each other, but they can hear, and that's enough to make them smile as they imagine each other's facial expressions and body language. Having previously established a good friendship, they're now able to communicate happily using only one of their five senses. And they're doing it without benefit of any physical connection other than air.

Later Jeb goes back out on the porch and resumes reading his comic. It's an old one, a collector item, printed before he was born. The creator of the comic died five years ago. But his vision, embodied in bright-colored ink on cheap paper and held together with two rusting staples, communicates joy and laughter to Jeb even though they've never met and never will.

In all of these cases, physical beings (Jeb, Sparks, Randy, the comic book guy) communicate with one another in ways that seem as natural as breathing. But when you take a close look at what happens, you begin to realize that what's going on is essentially spiritual: one spirit sending out vibrations which rouse the interest of another, which in turn vibrates back.

There is a mystery here, and we ignore it daily.

Another example: we e-mail one another from moving platforms such as cars and trains and airplanes. We have no physical point of contact—no connecting wire—nor do both parties need to be present simultaneously in order to communicate. The sender's car or plane could crash, killing him and destroying his laptop, yet the message, kept "alive" in the receiver's computer by dancing magnetic impulses, could eventually reach its target.

Still another instance of nonsynchronous but successful communication occurs every time we study a painting, or run a hand over the arm of a well-formed chair, or stare in wonder at an ancient sculpture. Here the communication is nonverbal as well as nonsynchronous. The person who painted the painting or crafted the chair or chiseled the stone may long ago have turned to dust, but the message of beauty or excitement or utility built into the work stays alive as long as there are people who can appreciate and respond to it.

One of the downsides of our time in history is that we're conditioned to think scientifically, which means, for most of us, physically. We think the world is a material place, explainable purely in terms of atoms and quarks, and that notions of spirituality or meta(*beyond*)physics are outdated or belong only in the realm of religion.

But the universe is as much home to spirit as matter, and depends on both dimensions for its ongoing function. Ancient generations sensed spirit in trees and animals, in feathers and rocks and blood. Einstein, Schrödinger, Heisenberg and others showed that elementary particles aren't particles at all, but rather "sets of relationship" that reach out to everything else in the universe. It may well be that spirit "drives" matter and that without spirit, everything would literally grind to a stop, or possibly cease to exist.

Whatever the connection between the two, it's sadly true that we don't see what we've not been taught to look for, or, seeing, explain it as fluke or misperception, thus reducing the multidimensional wonderland around us into a drab and mechanistic flatland.

Fortunately, Jeb and Sparks know better. To them, as to most kids and dogs, the world remains a fascinating place, shot through with telepathic mystery.

Jeb looks up from his comic book and smiles. Sparks opens one eye and, sensing joy, thumps the ground with his tail. No words, no wires, no worry. Case closed.

Voices of Hope

There are many signs of spring.

This loveliest of seasons signals her return with arrowing flocks of waterfowl, shy blossoms of tiny flowers, the flourish of raindrops drumming on roofs. For each of us, one event in particular signifies beyond doubt that spring is here. The sight of the first robin; the sound of geese honking in the night sky; the smell of thawed earth.

For me, the guarantee is verbal—the song of frogs issuing from the homestead marsh. "Song" is a tad too poetic, I suppose. The sound is more like the discordant tuning of an orchestra before the symphony begins. But to my ears, the cacophony of a marsh full of spring peepers is a sweet sound in spite of itself—a sound that fills me with pleasure and a deep sense of the *ongoingness* of things.

Last year the strident creaking seemed especially important. During that year we experienced death and some serious illness in our larger family, events that shake your foundations and wring the joy right out of your heart. It was a sad and soul-searching time for us, a time when we needed all the support we could find. And right when we needed it most, we were privileged to hear a chorus of hope rise from the lowlands.

It is at times like that when I feel most fortunate to live in the north woods. It's true that one's spiritual base is not dependent upon geography. In theory, it doesn't matter where you live. But I find great solace in the woods and swamps and hillsides of this part of the world, and am thankful that nature here is not some vestigial, distant thing.

Here you are reminded every day that you are part of a much larger, more abiding community than that of the merely human. Here it is possible to see your own life in the perspective of the eons. Here you can cry your grief to the wind and the rain and the sunset—and find your sadness rebutted by an ancient cry of gladness from the marsh.

In fall the frogs burrow into mud and are, to our eyes, dead and buried. All winter they are mute, unmoving, gone from life. And then in spring—a resurrection! A crawling from the grave of many months and a triumphant song of celebration. "We're here!" they chant. "We're here! We're here! We're here!"

For centuries, mystics have proclaimed the seamlessness of life. There is no real beginning, no real end. The spirit roams the cosmos, clothing itself in various forms, part of the eternal One. In our time, physicists have peered behind the veil of matter and seen that there is really no such thing as mass, but only energy. Now they, too, join the mystics in proclaiming the endless circling dance of life.

The frogs sing truth. Their croaking voices bespeak hope. Death is not something to be feared, trembly though we may be. Death is but a doorway to a different room in the mansion of the universe.

171

Narrative

With or without your full-hearted participation, life goes on. In the year following Kia's death, our daughter-in-law, Sara, became pregnant with our first grandchild. That winter Claire's father passed on. Some months later our first grandchild, Levi, was born; red-haired, bright-eyed, unarguably brilliant. As we neared the end of the century, dire forecasts of doom began to permeate the nation. At the start of Y2K, claimed a host of Chicken Littles, the sky would definitely fall. Computers would seize up, the financial system would unravel, the machines on which our modern world relies and which, in turn, depend on digital guidance, would cease to function, and life as we know it would come to a whimpering halt.

Instead we segued seamlessly into the new millennium. The lights kept burning, the airplanes continued to fly, and Apocalypse Now became Apocalypse Not. The only area casualty was the hospital in Brainerd, which stopped admitting new patients the day before New Year's—not because of Y2K bugs, but because of flu bugs. At the stroke of midnight we toasted one another and the new year, took a sip in memory of loved ones now gone, and raised a second glass in tribute to the great north woods. The crazier modern life gets, the happier we are to live close to the earth in an area relatively unspoiled. There is solace to be found in the rhythms of nature. No wonder Thoreau, that clear-eyed mystic, said, "In wildness is the preservation of life." Without the example of nature's balance and intricate interdependencies, we have no model on which to pattern our lives. The more virtual the world becomes, the more that model is threatened, and the more we are at risk of damaging the biosphere which sustains us.

A Place Called Home

We Americans are a restless lot. Our country was settled by refugees from elsewhere, men and women seeking a better life or running from responsibility. History shows that their restlessness was rarely cured by simply getting to America. Most of our forebears sank roots only to rip them up and move again, driven by dreams of greater opportunity, richer soil, or an easier life.

This tendency, this itch to move, appears not to have abated in our time. I read a few years ago that the "average" American changes residencies every seven-and-a-half years. This, of course, is a statistical picture of things, possibly skewed by a small percentage of citizens who move more frequently than most. But it nonetheless gives indication of an underlying discontent that might help explain why we seem in so many ways to be a nation at loose ends.

Walking around the homestead this past weekend I was struck by how long it takes for a place to become "home." When we bought this land nearly three decades ago, the entire thirty acres was hip deep in logging slash. It took months of cutting and dragging and burning just to be able to walk around without tripping. Aside from the beautiful grove of Norway pines the logger had left standing, and a cluster of tamaracks in the lowland, most of the land was stubbled with sprouts of popple and alder. The newly bulldozed driveway resembled an open wound. The vehicles, tools, building materials, and other bric-a-brac we brought with us gave our new homestead a trashy, "Welcome to Dogpatch," flavor.

But year by year the trees gained in size and beauty and the scars from our intrusion began to heal over. Here and there we planted trees by the hundreds and shrubs by the dozen, and each season we learned many new things about our place.

We know now when to expect the osprey to return and when the frogs will start peeping again. We look forward to the mid-June laying of turtle eggs and enjoy the hatching of each year's clutches of phoebes and bluebirds and swallows and robins. We have become intimate with the humps and swales of our land, and know which hills to stay off of in the spring so as not to encourage erosion.

We are acquainted with the ways the winter wind will pile the snow across our driveway. We have learned where the springs in our lake are apt to make the ice weak. We know which slopes will be snow-free first, and which last.

Everywhere we go upon our land we can conjure memories of some previous experience: a fallen tree, a campfire, a tumble on snowshoes, where the tractor got stuck. We look at a place and see not just today but also many yesterdays—and we lay plans for many tomorrows. When we travel away, whether to a nearby town or to a foreign country, we are always delighted to return to this place that we call home.

As the years unfold we understand increasingly how fortunate we are to have a stable base from which to view things. We see now that home isn't just a place of refuge and comfort, but also a benchmark from which to take the measure of things. Home is a humbling place, teaching us the vastness of our ignorance. Home is the stage upon which our dramas are enacted, and our characters tested and matured. Home is no mere hat rack. Home is our laboratory and our seedbed and our bedrock.

At its best, home is the very stuff of life, the ingredient of which healthy, life-affirming nations are composed.

Tomorrow

People who live in cold climates know one thing for sure: fall is no time to dawdle.

Fall is when the chickens of procrastination come squawking home to roost. The dozen-and-one things you put off last month join forces with the hundred-and-two things you put off all summer and conspire to remind you of the major projects half-completed last May just before spring fever struck.

Remembering all these undone things makes you uncomfortably warm. The road to hell, you recollect, is paved with just the kind of good intentions you've been having for the past six months. But then the fever subsides and is replaced by goose bumps, for here in the northland perdition sports more icicles than flames.

For a while you stare out the window at the wind-sculpted drifts of unraked leaves. You think of all the tasks that, leaf-like, have piled up since spring, and you wallow for a while in that curiously enjoyable sensation called self-loathing.

But sooner or later you realize that regret is not enough. *Tempus* hath *fugit*; what's gone is gone. So you didn't repair the cracked window in June. So what? So you haven't checked your antifreeze. No sweat!

You turn your reproach inside out like a sock and the "re" becomes an "ap." The thing is to start somewhere. Anywhere. Just start.

Armed with a rake (or a wrench or a caulking gun) you surge into battle, determined to redeem lost opportunity. Three trips to the hardware store and one bruised digit later, you decide to stop for lunch. There is, after all, no point in overdoing. Now that the midday sun has warmed away the overnight frost, your earlier sense of urgency subsides.

In the afternoon, distractions abound. The blue jay honking in the oak tree. The southbound geese honking overhead. Your neighbor honking in the driveway, come to take you away to a football game.

Later that night you sit by the fire and reflect upon Aesop's tale of the ant and the grasshopper. Admittedly you have fiddled away more than your share of summer days, fiddled while others have worked. But what, after all, is the point of living if you can't take time to kick back now and then? Besides, there is always tomorrow. Tomorrow you will change your ways.

Tomorrow you will attack that list of critical tasks. You will get up early and limit yourself to no more than two cups of coffee before you leap into the fray. Tomorrow you will burn through that line of piled-up jobs like a hot wire slicing through marshmallows.

Tomorrow you will be disciplined and focused and relentless.

Tomorrow you will be invincible.

Tomorrow.

Midnight Surprise

I stepped outside just as a great horned owl hooed loudly from a nearby tree. I stopped and listened, transfixed, as a second owl, and then a third, replied to the first, and in a moment I was carried back in time to an eventful night some years ago; a perfect case of *deja-hoo*.

Back then we had laying hens, and normally we closed the chicken coop at dusk. That night I'd forgotten. My wife's folks had come to visit from Seattle, and naturally we stayed up late talking. Then, just before midnight, I remembered.

"Back in a minute," I said, grabbing a flashlight. "Gotta close the chickens up."

The night was cold, the stars enormous. I walked out to the barn, humming, glad to be alive. The outside door was open and I stepped inside. The coop was off to the left, next to the partitioned room we used for storing grain. The door to the coop was open and I started to go inside, then stopped abruptly.

On the floor before me lay a dead chicken. The rest of the flock stood ramrod stiff along the roosting poles, as if frozen at attention. Across the little room, diagonally from where I stood, a pair of enormous yellow eyes glared unblinking into the beam of the flashlight.

It took a moment to realize the eyes belonged to a great horned owl. They were so big, so unyielding, that I took an involuntary step backward.

For several heart-stopping moments we all stood motionless in the little room. Contradictory impulses collided in my brain. Fear, surprise, exhilaration; I wanted to run and I wanted to stay; I hated the owl for killing the chicken and loved it for its magnificent size, for its luminous yellow eyes, for the perfection of its plumage. So I stayed, eyes racing back and forth over the intricate black and grey markings of its breast, the sharp hook of its beak, the pointed tufts of its "horns." And all the while the chickens made no motion whatsoever, no sound, no evidence of breathing.

Finally I made myself step back into the other room. The owl, after all, was cornered. Standing in the doorway, I blocked its route of escape, and I'd heard a few stories about what the talons and beaks of great horned owls can do to human heads.

But what to do? The room was too small to maneuver around behind the owl, to force it out the doorway. I stood in the dark, trying to come up with a plan, when suddenly a crash and the tinkle of falling glass announced that the owl had found its own solution to the problem. From a standing start on the floor two feet away from the window, it had mustered the power to blast its way through a sheet of glass.

I walked back into the coop and stared at the hole in the window. The chickens remained at attention on the roosting bars. I stood where the owl had been, realized that its head reached to the height of my knee; and realized, too, that already I missed its wild presence.

Letting Out the Cat

Long ago, someone wise observed that life is habit.

From infancy on, we form patterns of behavior that we tend to repeat. For better or worse, those patterns join together to form the texture and the flavor of our lives.

Take, for example, the letting out of the cat.

Each morning of our lives, those of us who have been chosen by cats to be their masters are compelled to give them a hand, since cats have trouble with doorknobs. Some cat masters choose to install little flaps on their houses that are sized and designed to bypass the doorknob problem. But those of us who haven't are left with no choice but to play doorman.

This is where the habits come in.

The master (me) wakes from a warm and pleasing sleep into the rude world of 20 below. He sits for a moment on the edge of the bed reflecting on the temperature of the floor and upon the thorny responsibilities life has placed in his path. He thinks, fleetingly, about putting on his slippers, but instead responds to the ancient bathroom instinct and pads out into the hallway barefoot.

Emerging from the master litter box, he spies the cat arched against the new sofa meticulously unlimbering her claws. He hisses vile commands and the cat peers lazily in his direction. Her look communicates what her absence of language cannot. He stamps his bare foot on the hardwood floor, amazed at the pain this produces in his toes. The cat finishes digging her nails into the sofa and trots purposefully toward the door.

"Just a minute," says the master, bent over and rubbing his toes. "Just a lousy minute." He shuffles into the kitchen to start the coffee, wishing he'd put on his slippers. The floor feels like a sheet of ice.

He is reaching to activate the coffeemaker when the cat begins to complain. The urgency of her meowing distracts him and he moves toward the door. The cat is standing on her hind feet, scratching at the newly varnished door, wailing as if the world is nearing its end.

"All *right!*" says the master, his bowels congealing at what lies ahead. "Just a doggone minute."

He opens the door and the cat steps out into the unheated entryway. The sudden change in temperature causes goose bumps to rise on the master's skin. He reaches the outer door, takes a deep breath, and flings it open. "Go!"

The cat stands on the threshold looking out at the swirling billows of condensing air.

"Go on!" says the master urgently.

The cat looks up at him with patient contempt.

"Go *on!*" shouts the master, his self-control shot. "I'm freezing my buns off out here!" He tries to prod her with his bare foot, but she moves directly out of his way and his toes strike the doorjamb.

Foul words fill the air. Caticidal thoughts flood the master's brain. Just as he nears the breaking point the cat steps out onto the walk, and the master limps on blue feet back into the warmth, to sit on the sofa and wait for the coffee to brew, forgetting that he never turned it on.

Another day has begun.

The Salesman

A salesman called from Los Angeles and by way of breaking the ice inquired about the weather.

"It's cold," I said. "About twenty below. But sunny."

"You're kidding me," he said. "How can it be sunny and twenty below?"

"Arctic air mass," I said, trying not to sound too smug.

"Wow!"

I could tell he was really impressed, and I almost started in about how the trees crack at night and how the sundogs look in the morning sky but I held back, knowing it wasn't right to rub it in too much.

He recovered enough to give me his pitch about the stuff that was on sale this month, but I could tell his heart just wasn't in it. We were both pretending to be grown men, but the Tom Sawyer part refused to go away. What could he say to sunny and twenty below? Some silly thing about smog, maybe, or the latest freeway shootout.

Finally he gave up on the sales business and got down to the nitty gritty.

"How cold does it get up there?"

"Depends," I said.

"Depends on what?"

"On who the last guy is to tell." I was trying to figure out how to explain it as simply as possible. You're in the gas station in the morning and the first guy says he had 26 below last night and the second guy says 28 and the third guy (if he's feeling mellow) says he only had 25 and that leaves it up to the last guy, who rams it home at 30. But it was too complicated to explain to somebody from California, so I gave it up and said, "Never mind. Let's just say we're not overrun with cases of indecent exposure."

"God," he said. "It must be horrible to live up there."

"Yeah," I said, sighing. "It sure is."

"So what's it like in the summer?"

I sighed again. "You sure you want to know? It's your dime, don't forget."

"Not a problem," he said. "It's a WATS line."

"Well, first you have to understand about progressions, how one thing leads to another."

"Got it."

"OK. Up here we've got a basic sequence starting with poison ivy. Then it's poison ivy to ticks, ticks to mosquitoes, mosquitoes to tourists, tourists to deer flies, and…"

"Forget it," he said, sounding miffed. "I thought you were gonna be straight with me."

"I'm trying."

"Yeah, right." I could tell he was mad. From the ensuing silence I knew he was cooking up something nasty to say. Finally he spit it out. "Have a nice day," he said.

"You too," I said, but it was too late. The line was already dead.

Laughing at the Moon

Our grandson, Levi, like most young philosophers, is older than he looks.

Having recently logged his nineteenth month upon the planet, he's admittedly a long way from retirement, and grapples instead with issues like potty training and where not to draw with his beloved crayons.

But wisdom crops up in unexpected places, and despite the smoothness of his skin and the absence of a beard, Levi's something of a guru.

The other day, for instance, he grabbed my hand, tugged me out onto the deck, tilted his head way back, and waited for me to follow suit. Once I'd achieved the proper pose and was dizzily looking heavenward, he let go of my hand and said, "Sky."

Ah, yes. Of course. The sky.

I hadn't looked at the sky for months, other than to scan it for hints of impending weather. There it was, big as all get out, blue as a Norwegian's eye; a comforting tent that protects us from temperature extremes and dangerous radiation and the unnerving bleakness of outer space. I stared at the sky for a long time and so did Levi. Kids have a way of knowing what matters.

Mention the name of his cousin Tyler and he'll start chanting a mantra, "Tyla, Tyla, Tyla," as befits a religious devotion. At the venerable age of five, Tyler embodies all that's holy: the brute power necessary to remove an overzealous dog from licking your face; the mystical ability to ride a two-wheeler; the audacity to walk down the playground slide. As the reigning role model, he commands slavish respect and inspires single-hearted love. Would Levi consider ignoring his bosom buddy in favor of watching TV or putzing with Legos? Not likely. Friends deserve attention.

This ability to attend--to "be here now"—is what our young sage seems most intent on teaching us. We adults are many-focused, our thoughts and emotions scattered all over the place. We even pride ourselves on our ability to multitask. But youthful seekers of wisdom instinctively take the opposite tack. Do one thing at a time—and do it fully. There are moments when Levi, focused intently on a sight or sound or smell, literally screams with excitement, shouts for sheer joy, overwhelmed with the novelty of what stands before him.

This urge to celebrate the world rises anew in each generation, and is, I believe, a most precious legacy. To see the world afresh, to hear the music of the earth with unstopped ears, to sing and shout without embarrassment—these are gifts of immeasurable value, given freely and exuberantly by each newborn child.

One night, near dusk, my wife took Levi for a walk. They ambled hand-in-hand, listening to the chorus of cheeping frogs and the drone of mosquitoes, until abruptly he stopped and pointed toward the moon. He had no name for it, but it was there and he could see it, and the sight of it made him howl with laughter.

What a bizarre thing to see shining in the sky!

And what a wonderful way to spend part of an evening, laughing at the moon.

Narrative

Then, just as our lives seemed to be settling back into a pattern of quiet joy, terrorists destroyed the World Trade Center towers and plunged the nation into disarray.

A few weeks before it happened, my parents celebrated their 65th anniversary, and we'd been talking with friends who voiced the hope that the new millennium might prove more peaceful than the last. In the aftermath of 9/11, that hope dimmed. Just as my parents had struggled to make their way in a world mired in economic depression and edging toward war, so young couples at the start of the new century would have to deal with a fresh variety of international upheavals, the potential effects of which are anything but certain.

Happy Anniversary

The year was 1936—smack in the middle of the Great Depression. Millions of Americans had no jobs; millions more felt lucky to work a day or two a week. The prosperity of the Roaring Twenties was already a distant memory. The ominous rumble of war had begun to sound in Europe. A prolonged drought threatened to turn the American Midwest into a desert.

But hope—and love—spring eternal in the human heart. And Spike Nagel and Marie Behm were very much in love.

They'd grown up on the north side of Chicago a few blocks from one another, but never met until the previous Labor Day weekend. Spike was 25, a handsome, philosophical young man with a passion for baseball and a penchant for telling wry stories. Marie was 18, bubbling with energy, a determined and practical gal who loved celebrations and being together with family and friends. No money? No problem. They'd find a way.

So it was that on Saturday, August 29, they went to church, together with their best man and maid of honor, and took the vows of matrimony, promising one another to stay faithful and constant through thick and thin, after which they repaired back to the Behm residence on Ashland Avenue for the marriage feast and an evening of festivity.

One hundred guests graced the house that night, savoring slices of home-cooked roast beef and eating their way through mounds of homemade potato salad. After the feast, the rugs in the dining room and parlor were rolled back and an accordionist began playing waltzes and polkas.

Given the leanness of the times and the added constraints of Prohibition, you might imagine the party was rather subdued—but you would be wrong. Since Spike worked as a pricer in the liquor division of a large pharmaceutical firm, he managed to secure a case of bourbon and a case of gin, each "for medicinal purposes only." Working together well in advance of the wedding, family members had scoured the neighborhood for empty liquor bottles that still bore their labels. Then, with the help of a small funnel, they transferred the generic booze into more prestigious containers, stacked the bottles on the shelves above Grandpa's basement workbench, and set up a 2x12 plank as a bar, complete with a thick wooden curtain rod as foot rail.

The results were memorable. Even as a teenager, a quarter-century after that night, I recall ageing relatives growing misty-eyed with joy at the memory of sipping Old Taylor and Jim Beam and other hard-to-obtain libations in the cool comfort of the basement on that hot August night, while upstairs the house trembled with the laughter and steps of the dancers.

Thus began a union that has weathered 65 years and dozens of setbacks with amazing grace and stability.

Thanks to the megalomania of an Austrian housepainter named Adolf Hitler, my father went off to war shortly after I was born, and Mom had no choice but to return to the workplace. After he returned, the family grew steadily, until at length there were five of us kids. But shortly after the last one was born, Dad suffered a heart attack, and once again Mom pitched in to help make ends meet.

Later years brought additional trauma, including open-heart surgery and a pacemaker for Spike, a cancer scare and ministrokes for Marie, a steady thinning of the ranks of older loved ones, and the heartbreaking loss of three grandchildren.

But through it all, and in spite of each misfortune, they've managed to stay together and to reach out steadfastly to others. Like so many of their generation, they've held firm in their commitment to a common purpose, and to the shared values of duty, honor, economy, courage, service, love of family and country, and, above all, responsibility for oneself.

In a recent book Tom Brokaw labeled them members of what he calls "the greatest generation any society has ever produced." Though I may be biased, I can't help but agree.

Happy Anniversary, Mom and Dad.

May the path ahead be gentle, and the light shine down and bless you both.

Narrative

As if to remind us to keep focused on the positive, our second grandchild, Grace Ann, slipped into the world early in 2002. She gave us a scare early on when, at the age of two weeks, she contracted a respiratory virus and had to be airlifted to Minneapolis. For a whole week her little life hung in the balance—and then she began to heal, which made us delirious with joy. Two months after that, my father died at the age of 91, and once again joy turned to sadness.

A few years later the pattern repeated itself, but in reverse order. My wife's brother, Jack, succumbed to a heart attack a couple of weeks before our third grandchild, also named Jack, was born. Is there, I wonder, some cosmic form of bookkeeping that works at balancing our emotional accounts? The older I get, the more I'm aware of the steady oscillations of what the Taoists call the pairs of opposites: light and dark, warmth and cold, gladness and grief. I see now that each quality can only be defined by its opposite, and that each pair is unbreakably linked. And I've begun to appreciate the wisdom of Kahlil Gibran, the poet, who insisted that the further we're hollowed out by grief, the more joy we can contain.

Amazing Grace

During the wee hours of March 6, 2002, a miracle occurred: a child named Grace was born.

"Miracle?" you say. "What's so miraculous about that? Kids are born all the time."

You're right about the second part. In the twelve years prior to the year 2000, our planetary population swelled by an additional billion human beings, or nearly one hundred million newcomers per year. Considering those who passed on during that time, the number of new arrivals is actually much larger: probably more on the order of 175,000,000. Divide that by the number of days in a year, and you get an average daily arrival rate of nearly 500,000.

So what's so special about Grace?

She's my granddaughter, for one thing.

Naturally, I've been experiencing acute swelling of the chest and persistent attacks of giddiness: the old Overweening Patriarchal Pride Syndrome (OPPS). But aside from my own button-busting joy, there are several things about Grace that mark her as miraculous.

Her hands, for instance. Next time you're with an infant, put out your finger and let that little hand grab hold of you. Study the caterpillar-sized fingers and the perfection of those impossibly small fingernails. Feel the strength, so disproportionate to size, with which those tiny digits grasp your own. Consider the awesome fact that somehow this little person managed to shape herself into a complete organism, ready to brave the world outside the womb, without benefit of written instruction or external advice.

Look at her ear. Exquisitely shaped, complex as an intricate seashell, and yet no bigger than your fingertip. Consider her foot. It's fully articulated, packed with dozens of separate bones, a precision machine ready to transport her when walking-time comes—and it's no bigger than your thumb.

Because the miracle of replication happens every day, our eyes grow clouded and unseeing. But the arrival of each new child is cause for reverent celebration: a renewal, each one, of the greatest gift in the universe, the gift of life.

Grace fits in the crook of my arm. Her head is smaller than my hand. She weighs less than a large dictionary. But her silken hair shimmers in the light like spun gold. Her dark blue eyes are full of mystery and charm. And her tiny heart beats steadily, setting down the rhythm of her coming dance through life.

In a time of troubled uncertainty, tinged with fears of violence and dark hate, the arrival of new life reaffirms the hope of peace and caring. Each new child brings the possibility of improvement to our muddled state. Reared lovingly, each may help heal the cankers of blood lust and greed and ignorance that deform our current world.

Each deserves our wholehearted encouragement and support. Each is a dream fitted out in human form. And each, like our grandchild, is an embodiment of elegance and promise.

Amazing Grace. You can't tell me she's not a miracle. Don't even try.

Life in the Now

Dogs do it. So do cats. And chickadees and red squirrels and whitetail deer and great horned owls. Little humans do it, too--but less often as they grow bigger.

All creatures on the planet share the universal trait of living entirely in the moment; all except one species—us.

Yes, you say, but that's because we're conscious and the other creatures aren't.

Conscious of what? Surely the dog loves to romp in the woods or curl up in a patch of sunshine. Clearly the cat is aware of pleasure, purring with joy as she nestles in your lap. A deer smells the hunter, not vice versa, and the hearing of the owl is estimated to exceed ours by a hundred times. In terms of sensory awareness, other critters make us look deaf, dull, and blind. To say they lack sentience is absurd.

No, you say, that's not the kind of consciousness I meant. Other life forms use their senses, and they use them very well. But they're not aware of past and future and have no real ability to foresee consequences. Only humans can do that.

Now we're getting somewhere. Where? Into the heart of the human problem. For whether it is true or not that other species don't differentiate between yesterday and tomorrow, it is certainly clear that we humans do, with a vengeance. And the chief thing we gain by so doing is to make ourselves miserable.

As infants we live entirely in the moment. If we're hungry, we cry. If we're content, we gurgle. Watch a little child at play and you can't fail to be delighted. He or she lives with incredible intensity, fully engrossed in whatever's at hand. In those rare cases where a grownup retains a childlike focus on the Now, we have the makings of a genius or a saint.

How do we go amuck? By setting up a mental construct known as time, and then arbitrarily dividing it into pieces: a second, a minute, a year, eternity. We commonly imagine eternity to be a very, very long time, an unending stretch of years, a million times a million forever.

But the mystic sees things differently. From Lao Tzu to Buddha to Jesus, the message is the same: eternity is not an awareness of everlasting time, but rather an awareness that is itself totally without time. The eternal moment is a timeless moment, a moment that knows neither past nor future, before nor after, yesterday nor tomorrow, birth nor death.

We have all had experiences, peak events, which seemed to lie so far beyond time that the past and the future melted into obscurity. Lost in a sunset, transfixed by the play of moonlight on water, floated out of time and space in the enraptured embrace of a loved one; in these instances, if we examine them closely, there is no time. Whenever we grow truly and fully alive, time disappears, for the present moment is a timeless moment, and a timeless moment is an eternal one.

Search as you will, you can't find, see, or feel a beginning to the Now. Nor will you ever discover its end, even when you die, since you won't be there to feel anything end. The outer forms of the present moment cascade by in bewildering succession, but the Now itself remains indestructible, untouched by what we have been taught to interpret as "time."

Erwin Schrödinger, the founder of quantum mechanics, put it this way: "Eternally and always there is only now, one and the same now; the present is the only thing that has no end."

Ralph Waldo Emerson looked at his flowers and said, "These roses under my window make no reference to former roses or better ones; they are for what they are; they exist with God today. There is no time for them. There is simply the rose; it is perfect in every moment of its existence...But man postpones or remembers; he does not live in the present, but with reverted eye laments the past, or heedless of the riches that surround him, stands on tiptoe to foresee the future. He cannot be happy and strong until he too lives with nature in the present, above time."

Don't we have memories, and don't we ponder the future? Indeed we do. But when we examine things closely, we see that memory itself is a present experience, and so is anticipation. We can't go back to the past, nor can we go forward to the future. We can only live now, in this moment, for that is all we ever really have—or need.

"In this moment," says a Hindu sutra, "there is nothing which comes to be. In this moment there is nothing that ceases to be. Thus there is no birth-and-death to be brought to an end. Thus the absolute peace in this present moment. Though it is at this moment, there is no boundary or limit to this moment, and herein is eternal delight."

When Jesus was asked by his disciples who is the greatest in the kingdom of heaven, he called to him a child, and put him in the midst of them, and said: "Truly, I say to you, unless you turn and become like children, you will never enter the kingdom of heaven."

In the Now of a child there is neither past nor future—there is no time. Said the Zen master Zeppo: "If you want to know what eternity means, it is no further than this very moment. If you fail to catch it in this present moment, you will not get it, however many times you are reborn in hundreds of thousands of years."

This Now is the peace that passes understanding, freely given to us all. This Now is eternal life. When we forget Now, our fears and regrets swarm in to darken our minds and trouble our hearts. When we "come to our senses" like other creatures do, we regain our rightful place in the universe, and our lives are flooded with joy.

Now is all we really have—and all we really need.

Wabi-sabi

Tired of the endless quest for perfection?

Do you feel off balance, unable to meet the conflicting demands of work/family/personal growth/community service?

If so, you may find relief in an unlikely place—the Japanese notion of *wabi-sabi.*

Wabi-sabi emerged in the 15th century as a reaction against an era of lavishness, ornamentation, and ostentation, and through the centuries has taken firm hold as a deep cultural thread in Japanese thought. It draws on the insights of Zen Buddhism and Taoism, and has much to offer the modern troubled spirit.

Put simply, wabi-sabi is the art of finding beauty in imperfection.

It's the acceptance of things as they are, the celebration of that which is flawed and worn and authentic. It's everything that today's mass-produced technology-driven culture isn't. It's a mood of attentive melancholy, of seeing the fleetingness of things, of abandoning the search for permanence.

Wabi-sabi helps you see the world afresh and encourages you to embrace the moment. It gives you permission to value that which is weather-worn and bent from use, and to take delight in scratch marks and scars and rust—not because such things are superior to the shiny and new, but because they help us grasp the fact that all things are incomplete and subject to decay.

Relax, says wabi-sabi. Enjoy the moment. Proclaim the beauty of liver spots and wrinkles, of that which is pitted and chipped. Abandon the notion of "finished." When is a plant complete? When it flowers? When it goes to seed? When the seeds sprout? When everything turns to compost?

All comes to nothing in the end. Lightning strikes the mighty oak and drops it to the ground, where it dissolves back into earth and air. The wondrous works of man deteriorate, board by board and brick by brick, till at last there is mere rubble. Cell by cell our bodies move toward death, as cell by cell new bodies form to occupy our place and take life a generation farther.

Wabi-sabi celebrates signs of use and decay in order to help us understand that all things, including ourselves, are impermanent, imperfect, incomplete—and that that's okay. It's safe to trust the process and not worry about the result.

As such, wabi-sabi serves as a quiet foil to the raucous claims of our consumer culture, where the sleek and shiny and "new improved" are said to bring us the greatest pleasure, and where anything old or used is presumed worthless, or sharply reduced in value. It invites us to enjoy where and who we are without the need for relentless shopping.

By embracing imperfection, it leads us toward a place as special as old slippers and a worn flannel shirt—a place called peace of mind.

Treasure Hunt

M any years ago, when our son and daughter were in grade
school, the prospect of approaching Christmas filled us
with mild dread.

We were, to put it simply, dang near broke. Financially speaking,
the preceding year had not been kind to us. Now it was time to put
lots of presents under the Christmas tree and we hadn't the means
to do so.

The kids, bless their hearts, had made their wishes known. Our
son, deep into visions of small-game conquest, wanted a fiberglass
bow and some arrows. Our daughter, a lover of games, craved
electronics: an Atari, on which to play Pac-Man and Frogger.

Days ticked by and we grew increasingly uneasy. Yes, we agreed,
we can afford the main gifts. But what about all the other stuff? We
can't just give them one present each. That's not the American way.

Then, in a burst of true inspiration, my wife suggested a solution.
Why not set up a treasure hunt? We could wrap up a few small boxes
with little gifts—mittens, a pair of socks, a Hardy Boys mystery—to
put beneath the tree. But we could hide the main gifts somewhere else

and lead the kids to them with a series of clues placed in envelopes, each containing directions to the next, preplanted in their proper places around the house.

I'll never forget the excitement of that Christmas Eve.

At first the kids were clearly worried. A few meager boxes and two envelopes did little to ignite big dreams. But when they found mysterious notes directing them to "take twelve steps toward the kitchen and look up," or hinting that "there may be more beneath the sofa than just dust bunnies," they grew wide-eyed with excitement.

The further they went, the greater their joy. Instead of racing about from clue to clue, they took their time, savoring the prospect of what might lie ahead. And when at last the hunt culminated in the longed-for bow and game player, they both said it was the best Christmas they'd ever had. We agreed.

Pushed by adversity, we'd stumbled onto an ancient truth: anticipation trumps arrival. The journey is just as important as the destination; sometimes more. Whether making a living or making love, growing a garden or rearing a child, the process matters as much as the goal. Getting there is half the fun.

In the years since that joyous night, I've tried to keep the lesson in the forefront of my brain. From time to time I forget, and focus only on the actual treasure; and whenever I do, the riches lack luster.

Then I remember, and vow to regain balance.

Life is a treasure hunt—and the hunt itself is a sizable part of the prize.

How To Be Lonely

I s the human race getting you down?

Are you sick and tired of other people's stupidity?

Do you find yourself looking backward to the good old days, and wishing people were as decent now as they used to be then?

If so, you might consider retiring from the affairs of mankind and withdrawing into loneliness. To speed you on your way, I have drawn up a list of tested tactics, which if followed will nearly guarantee that you will end up where you wish to be: alone.

Shun human encounters. Don't put yourself into unnecessary social situations. Avoid looking at others. Never introduce yourself to a stranger. Don't write letters. Don't return phone calls. Be aloof.

Feel sorry for yourself. Lord knows, we've all got plenty of things to feel sorry about. Pick out a few of the worst things that have happened to you and dwell on them. Try to accentuate the negative. If something goes well, disregard it. Always imagine the worst.

Be unenthusiastic. People always react positively to enthusiasm. By being unenthusiastic, you will gradually but inevitably turn others off. Try not to get interested in anything. Remind yourself as often as possible that you are bored.

Watch plenty of TV. This is an excellent way to dull your mind, avoid real encounters, and strengthen your conviction that the world is going to hell in a handcart. The more you watch, the better. TV increases passivity, distorts reality, and gives you a perfect excuse for being alone.

Cultivate your regrets. Since everything you regret happened in the past (i.e., the good old days), dredging up your regrets allows you to avoid getting distracted by today and keeps your mind safely concentrated on the things that are beyond your power to change. A handy exercise is to list each regret on a 3x5 card, and then arrange and rearrange them into various patterns, to see which pattern depresses you the most. If the regrets get boring, you can always play Solitaire.

Take poor care of your health. Try to diminish your natural powers. Since the mind and body are interdependent, undermining your physical health can help dull your interest in the world around you, thus setting up a downward spiral in which your health deteriorates further because of mental torpor.

Try not to smile. This is extremely important. All the efforts you have made to isolate yourself from the human race could be wiped out by a single spontaneous smile. To guard against such a thing ever happening, practice holding your upper lip firmly between your teeth, and spend some time each day sucking on lemons.

If following this simple regimen fails to produce the desired effect of separating you from your fellow man, don't give up hope. Instead, become a fanatic.

Any cause will do.

Two Rules

Some years ago a fellow named William Least Heat Moon wrote a book titled *Blue Highways*. In it he chronicled his travels down the byways and back roads of America—the kind of roads that many maps depict in blue ink.

By sticking to roads less traveled, the author hoped to encounter rank-and-file Americans, people without pretense or great wealth or fame, the regular folks who make up the bulk of our citizenry. And find them he did: waitressing in cafes, clerking in hardware stores, wrenching on engines, tending the farm.

Each, he found, had an interesting story to tell.

But the most interesting of all to me was the Native American teenager he met in Utah, a Hopi named Kendrick Fritz.

When pressed to explain his values and beliefs, the young man responded by telling about the Spider Grandmother, the Hopi version of the Great Spirit.

"The Spider Grandmother gave two rules," he said. "She gave them to all peoples, not just Hopis. If you look at them, they cover everything.

"She said, 'Don't go around hurting each other,' and she said, 'Try to understand things.'"

In the dozen or so years that have passed since I first read *Blue Highways*, I have often pondered the wisdom and applicability of the Spider Grandmother's rules. Time and again I have found them right on target.

The first (roughly parallel to the Golden Rule of Jesus) reminds you of the futility of anger and the wrongness of revenge, and keeps you aware that hurt can take many forms besides the purely physical. We can hurt one another with gestures, with looks, with lies, with gossip, with our tone of voice and even with our silence.

The second (without counterpart in our Judeo-Christian tradition) urges us to go beyond merely restraining our aggressions, exhorting us to make the effort necessary to see what the world looks like through different eyes. In a time when an alarming number of us seem contemptuous of viewpoints at variance with our own, this rule seems especially valuable. Any fool can disagree, but it takes genuine effort to try to understand what it is you're disagreeing with.

The root of this word goes back to the Old English *understandan*, which meant "to stand under;" to take a stance of humility and respect rather than one of arrogance or presumption. The impetus to understand grows naturally out of a sense of the sacredness of things, as does the urge not to go around hurting one another.

The young Hopi put it this way: "Our religion keeps reminding us that we aren't just will and thoughts. We're also sand and wind and thunder. Rain. The seasons. All those things. You learn to respect everything because you are everything. If you respect yourself, you respect all things."

Babee

During a recent cold snap, I whiled away some evening hours thinking about automobiles. Not automobiles in general, but automobiles I've known and loved.

The first one that came to mind, of course, was "The One I Once Owned and Should Never Have Sold;" my 1953 MG-TD. We've all had at least one car like that, and thinking about it is a painful delight. Like a teenage romance seen through the filter of several elapsed decades, the object of one's affection takes on a dreamy patina of perfection.

In the case of the MG, what I recall is the thrill of the wind in my face and the way people's heads swiveled when I drove into town. Small boys would sidle up and ask, "Is that a race car, Mister?" Pretty girls would smile. Old men would get a gleam in their eye, jolted back in memory to visions of a Model A roadster stripped down and ready to scream.

Now I know, intellectually at least, that Babee (which was her name) had flaws. She was powered (actually, quite underpowered) by a very small four-cylinder engine. Going downhill with a tornado behind you would net maybe 80 mph. In the company of Corvettes, Babee felt ill at ease. And there was that nagging problem of the sagging doors. MG bodies of that vintage sported skeletons of oak, not steel; and as the years wore on, their door frames had a nasty but understandable habit of slumping earthward.

Then, too, there was the annoying gap that formed above the top of the side curtains when you drove over 30, a gap which allowed the great outdoors into the interior of the car. No worry during summer, but vexing to the extreme the other eleven months of the year.

But problems such as these were minor. And they were utterly offset by the gifts that Babee lavished upon her owner. The way her fenders flared, flowing like liquid up and over and down and away from her wheels. The glitter of her chrome radiator housing, topped by the heavy octagonal radiator cap. The jaunty look of her little windshield jutting up behind the stately length of her engine bonnet. The rhythmic spacing of the louvers in the bonnet, and the way it lifted up, folding out of the way like the wing of a bird or a butterfly. The warmth of her wood-trimmed steering wheel in your hands. The polite little cough she made when you turned the key and tugged at the starter knob. The tremor of her revving engine and the rush of watching her tach needle bounce to the right.

And finally and ultimately, the thrill of guiding her over the open road with the top down and the wind in your hair and the sensation of being in flight. Babee offered sensory delight coupled with four on the floor and a suspension system that made you lust after roads with curves. Cuddled in her soft leather seat, so low to the ground you could hang your arm over the side and almost file your fingernails on the passing pavement, you knew as you drove that driving itself was sufficient reason for being alive. It didn't matter where you were going or why. What mattered was feeling the pulse of the car beneath you and the blessing of the sun upon your face.

What mattered was the ride.

Roadside Wisdom

Readers of a certain age can close their eyes and visualize a procession of small red signs with white letters bordering the two-lane country highways of their youth, before the era of Interstates.

The signs usually came in clusters of five, spaced about a hundred feet apart, bordering a farmer's field. Each of the first four signs contained one line of a rhymed verse, and the fifth identified the sponsor of this outdoor poetry, a popular shaving cream called Burma-Shave.

SHE KISSED THE HAIRBRUSH
BY MISTAKE
SHE THOUGHT IT WAS
HER HUSBAND JAKE
Burma-Shave

The signs were the brainchild of Alan Odell, son of Clinton Odell, the founder of the family-owned company. The first signs were put up in 1925, on the outskirts of Minneapolis, and soon spread to the rest of the country, continuing as American landmarks until the 1960s. The precursor to modern billboards, they provided an interesting diversion on long trips, and quickly became a part of popular culture.

THIS CREAM MAKES THE
GARDENER'S DAUGHTER
PLANT HER TU-LIPS
WHERE SHE OUGHTER
Burma-Shave

SAID FARMER BROWN
WHO'S BALD ON TOP
"WISH I COULD
ROTATE THE CROP"
Burma-Shave

Some of the signs included messages about driving safety, though to read them you had to take your eyes off the road.

IF DAISIES ARE YOUR
FAVORITE FLOWER
KEEP PUSHIN' UP THOSE
MILES-PER-HOUR
Burma-Shave

AROUND THE CURVE
LICKETY-SPLIT
BEAUTIFUL CAR
WASN'T IT?
Burma-Shave

But most of the signs gently touted the advantages of using Burma-Shave, or the woes that might betide the man who didn't.

TO CHANGE THAT
SHAVING JOB TO JOY
YOU GOTTA USE
THE REAL McCOY
Burma-Shave

GRANDPA'S BEARD
WAS STIFF AND COARSE
AND THAT'S WHAT CAUSED
HIS FIFTH DIVORCE
Burma-Shave

At the peak of their popularity in the '40s and '50s, some 7,000 sets of Burma-Shave signs picketed the sides of American highways. Annual contests encouraged citizens to submit slogans, with winners receiving a $100 prize. Some contests received over 50,000 entries. But the building of the Interstate system, the gradual rise in speed limits, and the appearance of much larger billboards spelled the beginning of the end, and in 1963 the company was sold to Philip

Morris. Shortly thereafter, the Burma-Shave signs were discontinued, and soon removed from their place in the rural landscape.

For those of us who eagerly read their lines of roadside wisdom, the memories live on.

DON'T STICK YOUR ELBOW
OUT SO FAR
IT MAY GO HOME
IN ANOTHER CAR
Burma-Shave

PAST THE SCHOOLHOUSE
TAKE IT SLOW
LET OUR LITTLE
SHAVERS GROW
Burma-Shave.

Narrative

Nearly half a century has passed since I first fell under the spell of the northern forest. Living here has proved an instructive adventure. I no longer believe that one particular style of life is more authentic than another; I think it's more a function of how truthful you are with yourself. I'm confident that happiness is portable, and that it's mostly a matter of choice. Life in the woods is not for everyone. And life in the woods today is far more sophisticated than it used to be. But being in touch with the seasons, hearing the rifle-shot of trees riven by frost-cracks at 30 below zero, feeling the warmth of the spring sun on the back of your neck, inhaling the perfume of pine resin, and marveling at the night sky in a place where ground light doesn't block your view of the stars all conspire to make me very glad to live where I do. I hope the bringers of so-called progress will think twice before they burden us with much more change. Convenience is a two-edged sword, destroying as much as it improves.

No Place Like Home

Not too many years ago, I dreaded the annual arrival of winter. The snow, the cold, the anemic sun, the moan of wind against the house; all seemed to conjure a foretaste of death.

During that period I came close to driving my family crazy with endless talk about moving. Minnesota, I said, was the pits. Minnesota was a paradise for fools. The north woods was one large asylum for the down-and-out, the weak of mind, the don't-know-any-better.

Gradually talk turned to action. We took a series of trips. We went to Washington and Oregon and northern California. We went to Florida. We went to Vermont and New Hampshire and Maine.

A pattern formed. On each trip we would leave the North Star State with manic joy, ecstatic at the prospect of warmth and sunshine and a promised land. For days we would drive and visit and marvel and talk, reveling in the wonders of Pacific beaches or the majesty of redwoods or the miracle of orange trees. We would collapse into our motel beds exhausted, heads swimming with visions of how good life would be wherever it was we were at the time.

Then, little by little, we'd begin to talk about home. Wonder how our friends were doing, wonder if the dog was all right in the kennel, wonder if the plants were getting enough water and if the chickadees were finding enough seeds.

Each time when the hood of the car or the nose of the plane was once again pointed toward Minnesota, we would experience an inward surge of joy and a sense of relief, knowing we were on our way home. "Oh, sure," we'd say. "Oregon (or Maine or Florida) is great. Just think if we'd started out living there. We'd probably be happy as could be. But shoot, they don't have any birch (or tamarack or popple) trees, and the traffic is insane."

When we closed the last few miles and all the familiar landmarks appeared, we were much more excited than we'd been on the way out. "Look, there's a deer!" "Wow, a clump of birch." "Hey, there's the mailbox."

At the kennel the dog would nearly die of joy at our reunion. Once in the house my wife would go immediately to inspect her plants, touching their leaves and feeling the soil to see if it was moist. The kids would dash about inspecting their rooms and hugging the dog and telephoning their friends. And I would go to the fireplace and light a fire, and later, after the car was unpacked and the plants watered and the mail sorted, we'd sit by the fire and say, "It was a good trip. Just think—last night we were in Seattle (or Chicago or Sault Sainte Marie) and now we're back here in the woods. Hard to believe, isn't it? But you know, it sure is good to be home."

Ever since those years of discontent I've found it impossible to muster the sort of disgust I used to feel. Winter, I know now, is part of living up here, part of the fabric of what we call home. And as Dorothy said when she came back from Oz, "Auntie Em, there's no place like home."

Junk Mail Jujitsu

Every month, it seems, more junk mail finds its way to us. Years ago our mailbox held a piece or two of correspondence along with the customary bills. Catalogs and circulars were rare. Now they constitute the major part of our mail.

For a long time I suffered from this change. Having been schooled by depression-era parents in the thrifty art of saving things, I tend to hold on to that which comes my way—including, of course, all those catalogs.

In recent years, despite my upbringing, I have been trying hard to decongest my life. But throwing a perfectly good, expensively printed, full-color catalog in the wastebasket unread does violence to my innermost parts. It seems so wasteful, so frivolous, so wrong. "Save it!" whisper the voices of childhood. "Throw it!" barks the author of *Clutter's Last Stand*. It's a classic lose-lose situation, like having one foot on the gas pedal and the other one on the brake.

So, for months, I sulked and felt mistreated. Surely this incoming tidal wave of mail was being sent to punish me for some transgression. Could it have been for that time in boyhood when I planted several cherry bombs in the neighborhood mailboxes? But no—the U. S. Postal Service couldn't remember that far back.

Then one day I sat down with a newly arrived catalog and actually read through it. It was jam-packed with things electronic. Exciting things, marvelous things, gadgets that could "Glamorize Your Life" and make you the envy of your peers. I grabbed a pen and circled several items for possible purchase. Then the phone rang and I set the catalog aside and the next day my wife threw it in the recycling bin.

A few days later I curled up with another new arrival. This one was filled with woodworking tools. Again I used a pen to great advantage, saving myself hours of in-store shopping, making my selections in the comfort of my living room. By the time I was done drawing circles around tools, I was well on my way to having the best-equipped workshop north of Minneapolis. Unfortunately, my checkbook indicated I lacked the ten or twelve thousand dollars it would take to place my order, so I carefully put the catalog aside toward the day when my fortunes would improve.

Next came a wonderful catalog full of books, and I hurried to commence my armchair shopping. By the time I was finished choosing a hundred of the better selections, it was clear that my order would never fit on the measly form attached to the catalog so, in disgust, I tossed the whole thing into the fireplace.

Thus it was that I found a way to turn the proverbial lemon into lemonade. I hate shopping almost as much as I hate junk mail. By fusing the two things together, I have stumbled on a delightful way to spin some pleasant fantasies and save tons of money in the process.

It helps, of course, to have someone in the family who will discreetly dispose of your dream lists once you're done filling them out. Failing that, you can always hope that forgetfulness will work its ancient magic. But the cardinal principle—the rule that makes this system work—is that no matter how beautiful the illustrations or how boldly slashed the prices might be, you must never, ever, succumb to the temptation to actually order anything.

Fill out the forms. Salivate over the pictures. Daydream to your heart's content.

Just don't part with a dime.

Nobody Loves a Radical

Were we to rank all occupations, few would come in lower than that of the radical. Situated far below such roundly damned professions as politics, used-car sales, and journalism, the business of radicalism is held in near-total contempt.

And no wonder. The radical brings us bad news. He seeks to upset the status quo. He holds our cherished conventions up to ridicule. He commits the unpardonable act of asking us to think— and to think about things we'd rather ignore.

The very word bespeaks a down-and-dirty life. It derives from the Latin *radix*, meaning root, as in radish. The radical by nature seeks root causes. He delves down to the origin of things, sometimes with the hope of uprooting them so they die. He is by inclination an extremist, contemptuous of compromise, willing to throw out not only the bath water, but the baby and the bathtub as well.

In self-defense, we seek to discredit radicals by smearing them with unsavory labels such as "peacenik," "tax-reform nut," "tree hugger," "radical rightist," or "ivory-tower intellectual." Unfortunately, such labeling doesn't change what's in the package. In fact, it may only serve to egg the radical onward. Having been besmirched with verbal insult, the true radical may reason that he has struck a raw nerve, and so must be on target with his probings.

And in this he may be right, for it is nearly axiomatic that we protect most vigorously that which we are least secure about.

In the last several decades we have witnessed radical attacks on segregation, the war in Vietnam, the North American Free Trade Agreement, environmental degradation, abortion, the inequality of the sexes, big government, drunk driving, and globalism, to name but a few. In each case, defenders of the status quo screamed loudest where their arguments were thinnest. But out of these confrontations some lessons were learned—the best defense against the radical is first to ignore him and, if that doesn't work, to launch a counteroffensive as ruthless and devastating as possible.

What gets lost in all of this, and what admittedly is very hard to see in the first place, is that a radical of whatever stripe serves a valuable function. Given our proclivity to let things be, our tendency to operate from force of habit, it is necessary that our lethargy be punctured now and then, if for no other reason than to keep us all awake.

And it is precisely here that the radical excels. For he or she is the gadfly, the mosquito, the no-see-um that irritates us into action. By bringing things to our attention, the radical initiates the chance of change. By pestering us to choose sides, to say yes or no, the radical forces us to think. By refusing to desist until change is effected or his own voice is silenced, the radical forces society's hand.

Nobody loves a radical. Radicals bring turbulence, anxiety, pain. But without them, the U.S. would still be a colony of Great Britain, blacks would still be enslaved, women would be unable to vote, there would be no fair-labor laws, DDT would still be sprayed upon the land, and, for all we know, the war in Vietnam might still be dragging on.

Stone Lessons

For most of the past three decades, I have made my living building things of stone. Fireplaces, barbecues, planters, retaining walls, walkways, veneer walls, even the occasional house.

Every day, except for the toe-nippers of winter, I spend several hours in the company of rocks, sorting them, washing them, splitting and trimming them, loading them into trucks, and eventually laying them in a wall. It's not very glamorous work. My fingers get pinched, my back gets bent, and sometimes my attitude gets surly. But out of it, in addition to food on the table, come objects of usefulness and, hopefully, beauty.

And, little by little, some insights.

High on the list of these lithic lessons is the importance of making haste slowly. There is no possible gain in trying to hurry a rock. Every time I have sought to race through the working day, something has gone wrong. It's as if the stones object to my frenzy and show their displeasure by squirming around or even falling out of the wall. "We will not be rushed," they seem to say. "There's plenty of time to do things right. Calm down."

Which, given their age, makes good sense. The stones here in northern Minnesota are among the oldest on the planet, ranging in age from 2.5 to 3.3 billion years! The commonly held age of the planet itself being 4.6 billion years, one can see why our local stones are in no big hurry.

A second major lesson is that the solution is inherent in the problem. Faced with the question of where to place a given stone, I have found almost invariably that the stone itself will pick its own spot if I can just manage to keep my ego out of the way. Instead of forcing an answer to the question, you just need to study the problem carefully, confident that the solution will in time reveal itself.

Which leads on into lesson three: each stone is unique. There's no such thing as an "average" stone, just as there are no average oak trees or turtles or chickadees or people. Each is a one-of-a-kind never-before-and-never-again marvel. Nor do they remain static. Every moment, day and night, a stone loses atoms to the air or water or dirt around it, and in return takes on new atoms from its surrounding matrix. If our own life spans weren't so pitifully short, we would be able to see the growth and change of the stones around us. We could watch them change size and shape and color and crystal structure, and we might even be tempted to think of them as having life. But since our years here are mere blips on the geologic screen, we tend to think of stones as being inert.

Finally, hanging around stones for all these years has shown me that your work reflects your soul. Ultimately, you can't hide a thing.

What you do and how you do it tells the world more about you than any autobiography could.

Whatever your line of work, if you don't do it right, it won't stand the test of time. And neither will you.

Sunshine Satori

W e've all experienced it: that sudden moment of insight when the scales fall from our eyes and we see, clearly, what before was hidden.

Zen Buddhists call it *satori*—a state of intuitive illumination. Since, to the Buddhist, the goal of spiritual seeking is enlightenment rather than salvation, experiencing satori is an important event. The entire body of Buddhist thinking insists that enlightenment comes when we learn to accept the now, the is-ness, things-as-they-are, and let go of previous mental constructs and emotional expectations.

When these moments of clarity come, you realize with an inward giggle that you are all right, that right now is perfect, that you don't need anyone or anything else in order to be at peace. If the moment of insight is powerful enough, it may lead directly to lasting enlightenment. If not, it may still prove a valuable step toward that goal.

Sadly, you can't manufacture such events. You can prepare your mind and spirit through meditation and simplification, as have thousands of monks and seekers through the ages. But such preparation doesn't guarantee that satori will occur. Like other gifts, it comes unbidden and can leave as quickly as it arrives.

When it comes, you know it. Afterwards the trick is to remember and to incorporate the insight into your daily life.

Last summer, while returning from a trip to Scotland, I had such a "light bulb" experience, and have been pondering its implications ever since.

We were flying over Ireland when it happened. Having attained cruising altitude of 37,000 feet, well above the clouds, the plane was awash with midday sun. But when I leaned against the window and looked down, I could see that the sky below us was roiling with dark grey rain clouds. We flew on and abruptly the clouds disappeared and sunlight poured down onto the green fields far below. A little farther and more clouds appeared, blanketing the land from view.

Suddenly I realized that to people beneath the clouds, the world appeared overcast and probably depressing, while those of us in the plane were only aware of sunshine. The difference in perspective was enormous. From below, the world was dark and irksome; from above, glorious.

In a rough sense, that's the difference between enlightenment and the absence thereof: once you punch up through the clouds of everyday events, you realize the sun is actually always shining.

Sadly, the insight is hard to sustain. When it fades, you go back to the prior mental notion of how things should be—but aren't— and it's bye-bye happiness. Most of us live most of our lives straining against just such circumstances. We tell ourselves that happiness will come later, after we can afford the new house or the nifty car, after we have kids, after we get the promotion or the divorce or the inheritance, after the kids graduate, after we retire.

We live beneath clouds of worry and fear and longing and accept the clouds as normal and abiding. But many of the clouds are self-created, mere emanations from our troubled minds. Once we've accepted the clouds as reality, the shadows they cast are undeniable. This is not to suggest that life is without pain. But when satori comes, and the light breaks through, we understand the larger truth: above those clouds the world is bathed in constant sunshine.

Rural Entertainment

We push the canoe off from the shore, my wife in the bow, myself in the stern, my pant leg and boots redolent with the sweet ripe reek of swamp muck.

It's Sunday, the sun sleepy-warm on our necks, air still, sky luminous. Ahead stretches a miniature forest of wild rice stalks, greenish gold in the afternoon sunlight, stripped clean of their summer's production. The earthy-tasting kernels that we so dearly love to eat have gone to feed someone else, harvested by ricing sticks and windstorms, slicing rains and hail. That which humans did not take will find its way into the bellies of ducks, homegrown fuel to help propel them safely south for winter.

We glide through a flotilla of lily pads, some so large they jar the eye. They, too, have given up their summer's yield, and now seem glad to rest, recumbent on their giant waterbed.

"Look!" I sight past my wife's pointing arm toward a bittern, amazed at the lumbering wing beats and toenail-dragging takeoff.

A few minutes later we emerge from the vegetation into open water and rest our paddles across the gunwales. The canoe moves soundlessly forward, past the swirl of a fish, past a series of breaking bubbles, past a half-submerged stick. I look down into the water and instead of the water I see clouds floating by, and the reflected forms of four flying ducks. The upside-down world is hypnotic, serene. Here, I sense, here in the middle of this little lake, here is all the tranquility that one could ever need.

A glance at the far shore yields the further beauty of a tree line reflected in perfect symmetry with itself. It is no wonder that much Native American art is ordered along these lines, one side mirroring the other, one shape echoing its neighbor. From the vantage point of a canoe, the world appears as Siamese twins, sky and water joined to sky and earth.

We resume paddling and pass over the remaining open water into the rice bed again. The *tink* and *scree* of stalks against aluminum triggers the takeoff of nearby mallards and again we rest our paddles, marveling at the muffled thunder of their wings.

Then, rising white and magnificent from the cover just ahead, an egret pumps its way into the air and swoops with an elegant flourish onto a dead tree at the shore. Behind the snag stands a maple, its leaves already scarlet. The sight of the pure white bird against the glowing red tree is overwhelming. We sit for a long while in perfect silence, dumbfounded by the beauty and our own blind luck.

Later, as we paddle our way back to shore amid squadrons of ascending ducks, I find myself thinking of various friends from the city who have asked, through the years, what we do up here in the woods. And I can't help but wish they were here with us now, to sample a slice of our rural entertainment.

For the Birds

All winter we talked about building birdhouses and suddenly it was spring.

"Don't worry," I said. "There's still time. As soon as we get the garden plowed and the winter stuff put away and the summer stuff out and the grass seed planted and the firewood stacked and the garage cleaned up and the spruce trees transplanted, we'll build the birdhouses."

"But they're here," said my wife. "They're here and they're ready to nest."

Thus it was that I fell behind on my Master List. But the building of the birdhouses was fun. First a wren house (actually some mere remodeling of last year's house) and after that one for the bluebirds.

"But what about the chickadees? I thought we were going to have a chickadee house, too."

Back to the shop. "There. A custom-made home for the chickadees, built to DNR specs."

I mounted the chickadee house as high in the tree as my ladder would reach. When I got down I saw it was crooked.

"Look!" cried my wife. "Something's trying to get in the wren house."

The something turned out to be a tree swallow.

"Not to worry," I said. "The hole's too small for a tree swallow." I was going to say more but instead I went back to the shop. Half an hour later the tree swallow house was done.

"It says here the chickadee house should be on a post," said my wife.

I climbed back up the ladder and removed the chickadee house. When I got down the tree swallows were gone.

"They're going in and out of the bluebird house," said my wife. I wandered off in search of a long pole.

"There," I said, an hour later. "It's up on a post, the way it should be."

"Did you remember to put the sawdust in the bottom?"

Ah, yes. The sawdust. According to the DNR brochure, the chickadee house (now perched some twelve feet in the air atop the post) was supposed to have sawdust in the bottom. I was about to reply when my wife pointed toward the post. "Wrens," she said. "The wrens are going into the chickadee house."

I sighed.

"Honey, why don't you go take a nap," said my wife.

When I woke up, order had been restored. The bluebirds had moved into the bluebird house. The chickadees were nowhere in sight. The wrens had settled into the chickadee house, leaving the wren house unoccupied. The tree swallows were perched on the clothesline, waiting.

I climbed back up the ladder and installed the tree swallow house, taking pains to be sure it wasn't crooked.

By the time I returned from putting the ladder away, the swallows were inspecting the house. My wife watched them, enthralled. "Isn't it wonderful?" she said.

Narrative

We who live in the woods do so because we like it here. We didn't move here to make lots of money. We came in search of something far more ancient and important: a thing called peace of mind. As near as I can tell, that sort of serenity thrives best in an atmosphere of simplicity, community, and closeness to nature.

Tinker with any of those ingredients and you diminish the prospect of peace.

Cultivate them and you find yourself in a place called home.

Acknowledgements

A complete list of the folks who provided support, encouragement, and suggestions for the material in A Place Called Home would double the length of the book. During the quarter-century I've been writing essays, ideas have come from all sorts of sources, including (but not limited to) casual conversations, e-mails, tons of books, countless magazines, unexpected events in the wild, scraps of yellowed newsprint, and the random bubbling-up of memories. No writer would be capable of giving credit to all the people whose comments and insights have grown to bear written fruit. Nevertheless, a short list of those whose influence proved pivotal to the emergence of this book is certainly in order.

As mentioned in the preface, it was Keith and Martha Anderson, then co-owners of The Country Echo (which they later renamed The Lake Country Echo), who, in 1981, first invited me to write an opinion column for the newspaper. Their unflagging support through the succeeding years proved invaluable, as did the loyalty and encouragement of the Echo's longtime editor and later publisher, Lou Hoglund. Without their help, my column "The Cracker Barrel" would never have existed.

Regarding the conversion of the essays into book form, I am indebted to Pat Benson for her concepts and suggestions, including the subtitle "Moments from an ordinary life;" to Tenlee Lund for her patience and professionalism while editing the manuscript; to artist Stephanie Mirocha for the use of her watercolor "Northern Lights II" as the cover of the book; and to Dan Heise, author's representative at AuthorHouse, for his comprehensive knowledge and unflappable optimism.

Then, too, I owe a great deal to the dozens of friends and family members who cheered me on through periods of uncertainty, and to the thousands of readers who over the years have, through their kind comments and letters, provided the ongoing feedback every writer covets.

Finally, and most importantly, I want to thank my wife, Claire, for her computer skills, impeccable proofreading, vast and loving patience, and relentless intelligence and good sense.

Author Bio

Craig Nagel lives in the woods near Pequot Lakes, Minnesota, with his wife, Claire. He divides his time between writing, reading, traveling, sailing, building things of stone, and having fun with his grandkids. To date he's published over 600 essays and several dozen children's stories. He is currently at work on a novel.

Printed in the United States
88283LV00003B/1-111/A